JAZZ VIOLIN

By Matt Glaser and Stephane Grappelli

Oak Publications

New York • London • Sydney • Cologne

Photo Credits:

Front cover photograph of Stephane Grappelli and Matt Glaser courtesy of Matt Glaser

Flying Fish Records	Page 4
Anthony Pepitone	Page 29
courtesy of Stephane Grappelli	Page 37, 64, 136
Culver Pictures (Stuff Smith)	Page 41
Darryl Pitt/Encore	Page 116
Atlantic Records	Page 120

Edited by Patricia Ann Neely
Book design by Iris Weinstein
Cover design by David M. Nehila

Copyright © 1981 by Oak Publications,
A Division of Embassy Music Corporation, New York, NY.

International Standard Book Number: 0.8256.0194.0
Library of Congress Catalog Card Number: 80-82972

Exclusive Distributors:
Music Sales Corporation
225 Park Avenue South, New York, NY 10010 USA
Music Sales Limited
8/9 Frith Street, London W1V 5TZ England
Music Sales Pty. Limited
120 Rothschild Street, Rosebery, Sydney, NSW 2018, Australia

Printed in the United States of America by
Vicks Lithograph and Printing Corporation

Acknowledgements

This book is dedicated to Joe Venuti.

Thanks go to so many people:

First of all to Stephane Grappelli; without him, this book would never have come into existence. He gave unstintingly of his time and energy.

to Richard Green and Robin Williamson, who started this project years ago;

to Yehudi Menuhin, Jean-Luc Ponty, and Svend Asmussen for taking time from their busy schedules to give interviews and information;

to Steve Slottow, for help with the transcriptions and in general, his invaluable suggestions;

to Evan Stover, Stacey Phillips, and Joe Weed for contributing their fine transcriptions;

to Linda Neagley, my indefatigable typist;

to friends who helped with the music; Darol Anger, David Armstrong, Carter Brey, John Carlini, Paul Ehrlich, Phil Gaberman, Eric Levine, and Richard Lieberson;

to friends who helped with the text; Alan Senauke, Tony Trischka, and Diane Williams;

to the folks at Oak; Pat Neely, Peter Pickow, Jason Shulman, and Brook Hedick;

to Grappelli's managers past (Cliff Hocking) and present (Abbie Hoffer) for arranging interviews;

to Pat Cox of Atlantic Records for arranging the Ponty interview;

to Jan Albert of WBAI - *Pacifica,* for allowing me to print part of her interview with Grappelli;

to *Coda, Cadence, New Yorker,* and *Rolling Stone* magazines for allowing me to quote parts of previously published interviews;

and finally, to my parents, for more reasons than I can count.

Joe Venuti

CONTENTS

Foreword	6
Introduction	7
Menuhin Interview	9
Historical Background	12
Grappelli Interview	22
Stephane's Style	29
Bowing	30
Left Hand	31
Improvisational Style	31
Musical Language	33
A Table of Stephane Grappelli's Melodic Motifs	34
Reading a Transcription	38
Notational Symbols	41
Analysis of Six Jazz Violinists	42
It Don't Mean a Thing I	46
Oh, Lady Be Good I	53
Oh, Lady Be Good II	55
Dinah	58
After You've Gone I and II	63
Shine I	68
Shine II	71
I've Found a New Baby I	74
I've Found a New Baby II	78
I've Found a New Baby III	82
Sweet Georgia Brown I	85
Sweet Georgia Brown II	88
Baby	90
Undecided I	94
Undecided II	95
Undecided III	97
Undecided IV	101
Alabamy Bound	103
Sweet Lorraine	106
I Can't Believe I	108
I Can't Believe II	112
Sweet Sue	116
Ponty Interview	120
Appendix	127
It Don't Mean a Thing II	127
Sweet Georgia Brown III	131
Groovin' High	136
Cat Coach	138
Discography	142

fOREWORD

I'm sure that this book will help considerably the next generation of musicians who play jazz violin; not, in fact, to follow us in what we did before; *au contraire,* I hope they can find for themselves something new to do.

I hope that this book will give young people who want to play jazz on the violin some confidence, and help them morally —that somebody like me, who never studied the violin, can do it, then maybe they've got a chance themselves. For those who are really musicians, there is no problem, they always find their way; but I'm sure this book will bring them, with the musical transcriptions, considerable help.

Best wishes,

Stephane Grappelli

INTRODUCTION

   Welcome to a book which examines the work of Stephane Grappelli and five of his contemporaries: Joe Venuti, Eddie South, Stuff Smith, Svend Asmussen, and Jean-Luc Ponty. The particular focus here is on jazz violinists who play standards. Alas, the modern players will have to wait for another book.

   Contained herein are transcribed solos with analyses, interviews, biographical, and historical material, and a chapter on Grappelli's style. In addition, there is an appendix which contains, among other things, a discography.

   I sincerely hope you find this book valuable. Please feel free to write me with any comments you may have. Address all correspondence to Matt Glaser, c/o Music Sales Corporation, 33 West 60th Street, New York, New York 10023.

The use of the violin as a vehicle for improvisation is by no means a new development. Hungarian and Roumanian gypsies, American fiddlers, and Indian classical violinists all improvise to some extent as well as jazz violinists. In a broader sense, all musicians must bring some element of spontaneity to their playing.

World renowned violinist Yehudi Menuhin is well versed in dealing with the deeper implications of music. He's able to see the unifying threads which tie together seemingly diverse styles, and has recently become involved with improvisation through working with Ravi Shankar and Stephane Grappelli. I knew he'd be able to supply a brilliant overview of our topic and he was gracious enough to grant me the following interview.

MENUHIN INTERVIEW

Matt Glaser: *Mr. Menuhin, what role do you think improvisation should play in a violinist's career?*

Yehudi Menuhin: *Of course we all try to improvise to some degree. I mean even when we play classical works or works which we have studied from a score, we still try to bring an element of spontaneity and improvisation. But I think improvisation really belongs to music basically, and all folk music and unwritten music has always had an element of improvisation, like Indian classical music, or African music, or jazz. And that's what attracted me enormously to Stephane Grappelli, because he is a master of this kind of improvisation. There's no one, certainly on the violin, who improvises as freely and brilliantly and easily and imaginatively as Stephane does.*

MG *What was your very first experience improvising?*

YM *I've never improvised! That's why I've been so attracted to all of those who do; to Ravi Shankar and to Stephane Grappelli. From my earliest years I was trained to study already written works, and I'd love nothing more than to have that talent or to develop it, but the nearest I can get is to play with people who do, or at least I bask in their glory.*

MG *So, when you played with Ravi Shankar you played from a score?*

YM *Not always, but very often. What I'd do was, I'd often use a kind of shorthand where I'd write down the melody, the number of bars and what had to happen in certain places so I wouldn't get lost. But of course, if I had Ravi's training that wouldn't have been necessary. That's a very great discipline in training that the Indian classical tradition submits you to from earliest childhood.*

MG *Do you see a correlation between gypsy music and jazz?*

YM *Well, there is to the extent that there is improvisation although the style may be totally different. Grappelli of course, played with Django Reinhardt, the great gypsy guitarist.*
All of the great composers have always been fascinated by the improvising art in music. Brahms played with a gypsy from Romany and it was through him that he came to like the gypsy idiom and wrote those wonderful Hungarian dances which Joachim transcribed for violin. And then the "alla turca"—the various Turkish influences in Europe that also brought us food: the croissant and black coffee.
We've always loved the exotic; everybody who leads an ordered life would

like to have a taste of the exotic, the unpremediated, the adventurous, the unpredetermined; so you have to start with human nature. We need it both ways—we want security, we want to be able to say that tomorrow will be just like today, and at the same time we want adventure. Of course, it's very difficult to combine the two.

MG *Have you had experience playing with gypsy violinists?*

YM *I've met many gypsy violinists, but I haven't actually played with them; except for once in Budapest for a television show. There was this wonderful gypsy violinist there named Lajos Boros. I played for him two themes, one from the "Gypsy Airs of Sarasate" and the first "Hungarian Dance" by Brahms. He said, "Oh yes, those are old, old Hungarian tunes, but this is the way I play them" and it was something quite incredible. It was as if I had given him a skeleton and he clothed it in flesh and blood, and made it live and walk. It was quite exciting. That elaboration and ornamentation is something which defies description, you couldn't possibly write it out. It's far too complicated to write out—changes in pitches, changes in rhythm. You couldn't write out the subtleties with which he improvised on these themes.*

MG *But, when you're playing a concerto, don't you also have to make that leap from the written notation?*

YM *Absolutely. One has to make the leap from something which is outside of one to making it one's own. You have to appropriate it, it has to become one's own; that is a leap, and a tremendous one. You are quite right in stressing that, because any work that one plays, that has become one's own, has gone through that process, having been first notes on paper and then becomes something which is imbedded in your heart and your playing. But that is one thing—and that's the great thing—about literate music, Western music. We study great masterpieces and reproduce them, and give them to the public who knows them and expects them and so on. But it is totally different if we bring up something out of the race tradition, the tribal tradition. I mean, this Hungarian violinist was probably the tenth generation of violinists and maybe much more than that, maybe there's never been anything but violinists. Maybe they left India as violinists or string players two thousand years ago!*

MG *Mr. Grappelli constantly says that he hates to practice, that he never practices. . . .*

YM *He doesn't have to practice! Those musicians who play, who improvise—it's a totally different life. He picks up the violin and just plays. It's the difference between a painter, or someone who draws, and an engineer who makes blueprints. The engineer who copies the blueprints has to go back to the books and get all his instruments ready and his pencils and his compass and the plans for the building—how many cubic feet of plumbing and so on and so forth—and that's our life—the classical musician. But the painter, you give him a blank canvas and he sits down and paints. And that's the big difference and that's why, in fact, I long for this other freedom, but I am committed to one way of life, my way. But the nearest I can get to the other is to know painters—to know Grappelli and people like him who give me at least a little bit of that quality which* *of course used to be a part of Western music. Certain harpsichord players have that too, a man like George Malcolm—any harpsichord player who reads from a figured bass has to improvise, any jazz player has to improvise, and I'm trying to see that the children at my school get something of that.*

MG *In what way do you go about that?*

YM *Well, partly through figured bass and ornamentation and partly through composition. They all compose a little bit. I once came to the school and heard compositions by every one of the children, it was quite remarkable because each one composed according to his own temperament and personality. They were as different as they could be—it was very interesting. They get that at my school, which I think is a very important aspect of learning any art, in fact, learning to think. Because, if we're going to turn out automatons who can only repeat what they've read, and not even, having understood what they've read, then we're very poor people. We've got to have original minds who can improvise.*

MG *Can you briefly describe the recording sessions with Stephane and your impressions of them?*

YM *They were wonderful—great fun. I nearly always played exactly the same things, but he* never *repeated himself, but never—he couldn't if he tried. Each time we did a new take of the same piece he played something totally different.*

MG *How do you think he overcame the technical difficulties of the violin without a lesson?*

YM *Well, gypsy children play from their earliest youth imitating their father, or they take pieces of wood and make believe they're violinists— Suzuki begins that way at the age of three—it's perfectly possible. Because, just as with doctors, it's as dangerous to go to a teacher as it is to go to a doctor. If you can keep clear of them you're better off.*

hISTORICAl bACKGROUNd

"Jazz," proclaims the announcer on New York radio station WRVR, "is America's indigenous art form." And so it is. Specifically, it's urban American music and since American cities are melting pots, jazz could certainly be thought of as "melting pot" music. While retaining its identity as a primarily black means of expression, jazz can embrace many different styles, outlooks, influences, and nationalities. This universal aspect of jazz is the factor responsible for the somewhat unlikely phenomenon of jazz violin.

The violin began its jazz career as the black sheep in the family, the odd man out. It was up against a number of barriers, some psychological, some physical. In people's minds the instrument was strongly identified with either classical music or folk music; the classical bias found the violin being used as a **sweetner** in early bands, and the folk influence placed it in jug and skiffle groups.

There were other problems, too. The violin wasn't loud enough to be heard in most bands; it was easily drowned out by the horns. Finally, there were few men who could cut it; if they were classically trained they didn't swing, and if they could swing, their chops weren't up to par. (I hope you'll excuse these rash generalizations.)

However, in the early twenties a man appeared who had somehow reconciled this problem. He had tremendous technique, and he could swing more intensely than most horn players. When necessary he could produce enough volume to be heard in the midst of a big band, but he normally chose to organize small groups which were conceptually light-years ahead of their time. Finally, he had a personality powerful enough to persevere through all sorts of trials and establish the violin as a respectable jazz instrument. This man was **Joe Venuti.**

Joe was a combination of Paul Bunyan, Niccolo **Paganini,** and Louis Armstrong. A practical joker of Promethian proportions, Venuti did everything he could to frustrate would be biographers and obscure the factual side of his life. (Venuti jokes and stories are legend; for a small sampling see *Laughter from the Hip*, by Feather and Tracy.) For a long time he maintained that he was born September 1, 1904 on board an ocean liner coming to the United States from Italy. Later, data was unearthed that showed he was born in Lecco, Italy, near Milan; some say December 3, 1899, others say 1894.

Joe's folks settled in Philadelphia and started teaching him music when he was around four years old.

My grandfather taught me solfeggio. That's the Italian system under which you don't bother much about any special instrument until you know all the fundamentals of music. He would give me an orange, that represented a whole note. Then he would cut it in half for a half note. And then in quarters. He would change fruit every few days.

As a youngster, Joe studied the violin with Professor Thaddeus Rich. There's a delightful story which illustrates Venuti's constant devotion to the instrument. Joe, six years old, was playing baseball and it was his turn at bat. Suddenly, he threw the bat down and ran home. Explanation? He wanted to pick up his violin and play a tune that had come into his mind.

Early on, Venuti met his musical alter ego, guitarist **Eddie Lang.**

Eddie and I started to play together when we were in grammar school. You know, Eddie and I went all through grammar school together. We used to play a lot of mazurkas and polkas. Just for fun we started to play them in $\frac{4}{4}$. I guess we just like the rhythm of the guitar. Then we started to slip in some improvised passages. I'd slip something in, Eddie would pick it up with a variation. Then I'd come back with a variation. We'd just sit there and knock each other out. People would say, "What the hell is that?"

Joe and Eddie played their first real job together in 1921 in Atlantic City, less than two years after the first jazz recording was made. Shortly after, they became kingpins in what was known as *The White New York School* of jazz musicians. Their cohorts included Bix Biederbecke, Frankie Trumbauer, the Dorseys, Jack Teagarden, Red Nichols, Miff Mole, and the young Benny Goodman. Joe and Eddie became major studio sidemen, and played together in the dance bands of Paul Whiteman, Jean Goldkette, and Roger Wolfe Kahn. Between 1926 and Eddie's death in 1933 they recorded over seventy sides under their own names, with various combinations of musicians. Most of these cuts are chamber music jazz of the highest order, demonstrating Joe's impeccable technique, brilliant compositional mind, and intense proclivity to swing.

Shortly after Eddie's death in 1933, of complications sustained during a tonsil operation, Joe, although highly grieved at the loss of his partner, embarked upon a very successful English concert tour. He continued to perform with Lang inspired guitarists until the formation of the *Joe Venuti Big Band*, a rough-and-tumble organization that performed through the early forties.

At this point, Joe moved to Hollywood, where he spent the next decade living the anonymous life of a studio musician. During this period he also appeared on radio shows with his old crony from the Paul Whiteman days, Bing Crosby.

These were hard times for old-guard swing musicians, and Joe's career suffered. He relocated in Seattle, but spent most of his time playing the nightclub circuit of Las Vegas. Although forgotten by the jazz world, and a thoroughly obscure figure to the general public, Venuti nonetheless maintained the highest standards for himself musically and didn't permit his playing to deteriorate a bit. In the early sixties, Joe returned to Italy, his homeland, for a number of extended visits.

He was warmly received and recorded a sizable number of albums there, some of which are now available in the United States.

The late sixties saw an upswing in Joe's career which continued to gain momentum until his death in August 1978, This resurgence was due, in part, to the efforts of jazz promoter Dick Gibson, who sought Venuti out in Seattle and presented him at a number of jazz parties which were attended by prominent musicians. These people were invariably astonished to find that, not only was Venuti alive, but he was playing better than ever. This led to increased concert dates and a prolific amount of recording, mostly for Chiaroscuro Records.

Joe kept on playing until a few weeks before his death from cancer. I feel privileged to have seen one of his last engagements, at *Michael's Pub* in New York. He played three grueling sets a night, six nights a week, for a month. The up-tempo tunes swung vehemently and the ballads were played with searing intensity. Joe's sidemen (including such top brass as Milt Hinton and Bobby Rosengarden) looked to him with awe, love, and respect. Some of these guys were half Venuti's age, and by the end of each evening Joe had worn them out, but he was still going strong. As jazz mandolinist Jethro Burns remarked, "It's going to be many years before people realize how great he really was."

In one of his last interviews, Venuti told Jerry De-Muth of *Cadence Magazine,*

> Back in the twenties there were many fiddle players in jazz. But I was the first. There was nobody before me. After all these years, I'm still trying to prove the violin is adaptable to jazz.

All subsequent jazz fiddlers were tremendously influenced by Joe, if not by his specific style sense, then by his influence on their ideals. Venuti's playing opened the floodgates; soon jazz violinists, with their own distinct styles, began popping up all over. Among these, **Eddie South** was the closest to Joe in age.

South was born November 27, 1904 in Louisiana, Missouri. He began to study the violin when his folks moved to Chicago and it was soon to become evident that Eddie was a prodigy. He studied, at the age of ten, under Charles Elgar and later with Petrowitsch Bissing at the Chicago College of Music when he was sixteen.

Eddie began gigging at an early age. His first major job was as front man and musical director of Jimmy Wade's *Syncopators* in 1924. After leading this band for a number of years Eddie came to New York, worked for a while, and then left for Europe with singer Marian Harris. South remained in Europe to study the violin, first at the Paris Conservatory with Firmin Touche and then in Budapest with Janoz Deroz.

In 1937 Eddie made a number of recordings in Paris with Django and Stephane; these undoubtedly constitute the finest part of his output. (See "Dinah," "Sweet Georgia Brown," and "Eddie's Blues.") Shortly after, Eddie returned to the states and settled in Chicago. He played regularly on the radio in the forties and had a television show in the fifties. Eddie died on April 25, 1962 without having received the full recognition due an artist of his stature.

Eddie South was not at all influenced by Joe Venuti's style and of the violinists discussed in this book he is unique in this respect. His style was more classically based than Joe's, and less influenced by clarinet and horn players. In his later years especially, South's concern with rich tone and impeccable technique often took precedence over his jazz ideas, whereas Venuti's maxim always remained, "Swing, brother, swing!"

Venuti was supportive of Eddie South on a business level as bassist Milt Hinton recalls:

I came up under Eddie South, the great violinist, who Joe sort of sponsored, and this was back in the days when black musicians and white musicians were in separate ends. Even in those days he was one of those guys that there was never any stint of prejudice about him. Every time he played in a violin room he'd recommend Eddie South to follow him. He'd get there and there'd be a note in the piano from Joe telling a funny story for Eddie. It was really because of Joe Venuti that Eddie South got to play these very fine places.

On the other hand, Joe was less than totally enthusiastic about Eddie's approach to jazz on the violin. I once asked him about this and he just shook his head and said, "I like a man who swings."

His answer is not so puzzling when you consider that the violinists under discussion had invested great amounts of time and energy perfecting their individual styles to the point where they often became a little myopic. It's as if each had come to the conclusion that *he* had found the best way to play jazz on the violin, so why are those other guys playing like that?

Let's now turn our attention to a couple of jazz violin geniuses who were inspired initially by the muse of Venuti: Stuff Smith and the Great Dane, Svend Asmussen.

Writing in the *New York Journal American*, Louis Sobol, referring to the violin playing of **Stuff Smith**, said, "It caused pulchritudinous young women to let their hair down as they rose from their tables to the consternation of sedate escorts, and plunge into wild, uninhibited dances." Elsewhere it's been said that, "Stuff, pound for pound, was probably the most demonically, swinging musician in the annals of jazz."

Born Hezekiah Leroy Gordon Smith on August 14, 1909 in Portsmouth, Ohio, Stuff acquired his nickname as a teenager touring with the *Aunt Jemima Revue*. "There were so many people in the troupe and I didn't know all their names, so I called everybody 'Stuff'. Soon everyone called *me* 'Stuff'—and it stuck."

Stuff's father was a musician who built his son's first violin and taught him to play. Young Hezekiah (no wonder he got a snappy nickname) was taking classical lessons by the age of seven, but was soon influenced by jazz.

Joe Venuti and Eddie Lang came through our town and I snuck in with my dad, into a saloon, and heard Joe. "That's the way I'm going to play, Dad," I said, but he had other ideas for me. As it turned out, it was just Louis (Armstrong) who influenced me. I got some Venuti records, and they were pretty, but they didn't push me enough.

Louis Armstrong was my inspiration. I was supposed to be practicing classics, but I'd get my little victrola and go into the woodshed and listen to Louis. And practice Louis!

Smith's active early years included stints with the *Alphonse Trent Band* and a short stay with Jelly Roll Morton's group, which he left because his violin was inaudible in the midst of those loud horns. In 1936, Stuff found a solution to the fiddle's volume problem when he purchased one of the earliest electric violins.

Stuff and his sextet spent most of the late thirties in residence at the *Onyx Club* on 52nd street, where they were tremendously popular. After Fats Waller's death in 1943, Smith was chosen to lead the band, a post he held for only a short time before an attack of pneumonia forced him to quit. Moving to Chicago to live with his sister, Smith formed a brilliant trio with Jimmy Jones on piano and John Levy on bass. They went to New York and played the Onyx for six months. Jones left, and Stuff replaced him with Erroll Garner; when Garner left Stuff got Billy Taylor, and when Taylor quit, Stuff moved back to Chicago and opened a restaurant. "We served nothing but chitterlings, pig feet, fried chicken, and barbecue."

The next decade was not the best one for Stuff. He moved to California and worked sporadically until Norman Granz arranged a European tour in the fifties. Stuff collapsed in Brussels and underwent surgery in which the doctors discovered that his liver was about the size of a pea. This was the first of a series of habitual incidents: European tour, collapse, operation, and miraculous recovery. Under the wing of Baron Timme Rosenkrantz, Stuff spent most of the sixties in Europe and had quite a successful career between hospital stays. When he died in Munich on September 25, 1967, the doctors declared him a "Medical Museum."

Stuff Smith was an innovator. His approach to the violin was radical, bearing absolutely no debt to western classical tradition. Despite this fact Fritz Kreisler (a classical violinist) and he were good friends and ardent admirers of one another.

I've always visualized myself playing trumpet, tenor, or clarinet. Also, I don't use the full bow—only the end, about six inches. The reason for that is you can slur more easily, the way a horn would, and you can get more warmth. Using the end of the bow, moreover, causes you to bow the way you breathe. I mean it's my equivalent of a horn player's breath control. Then, if I want to make a staccato accent, I bring the bow up, but almost as if I were hitting a cymbal. I don't use too much vibrato, you can't afford to in jazz. Your thoughts and your notes come too fast when you play jazz. Accordingly, what you have to work for is what I'd call a balanced form of melody. Now you can't balance well if you have a straight tone followed by one with vibrato, so the best way, as I hear it, is to play straight tone all the way.

Finally, Stanley Dance in his wonderful book, *The World of Swing* quotes Stuff as follows, "There's one thing about the violin I'll tell you. You can swing more on a violin than on any instrument ever made."

Around the same time that Stuff Smith was playing with Jelly Roll Morton, a teenager in Copenhagen was absorbing Joe Venuti records and formulating a style of his own. Born February 28, 1916, **Svend Asmussen** began studying the violin at age six, and as a young man, studied dentistry and sculpture. However, after hearing Venuti, he devoted himself to jazz and was soon playing throughout Scandinavia with great success. Svend made his first recording in 1935 and two years later performed with Fats Waller and the Mills Brothers on their tour of Denmark. Benny Goodman tried, unsuccessfully, on two occasions to get Asmussen to come to America, but Svend has always been so popular in Europe that he has rarely felt the need to leave.

Svend, influenced by Stuff Smith in more areas than music, owned a restaurant called *Blue Heaven* in Copenhagen from 1940-43. During this period he appeared frequently as an actor and comedian. Asmussen's skills as an entertainer helped bring his phenomenal violin playing to a larger audience.

After the war, Svend began to perform with a sextet that drew record crowds all across Europe. Some of his recordings from this period have recently been reissued (see discography) and they indicate a peak in swing fiddling that is unequalled. On these sides Asmussen has the swing of Stuff, the fluidity of Stephane, the chops of Venuti and the harmonic imagination of Dizzy or Bird.

Svend has continued to grow musically and now plays everything from classical to jazz-rock, often on an electrified instrument with accoutrements such as a wah-wah pedal and phase shifter. His more recent records include *Amazing Strings* (where, through the use of multiple overdubs he appears as a small jazz orchestra improvising on classical themes and outings with Toots Thielemans and Lionel Hampton.

Stephane Grappelli was born in Paris on January 26, 1908. His mother passed away when he was three, and his father was forced to place him in an orphanage. (For more information about Stephane's early years see the complete Grappelli interview on **page 22**.)

Stephane's earliest memory of live music goes back to his sixth year, as he tells Jonathan Cott of *Rolling Stone*:

My father wanted to take me out of that orphanage, and since he knew Isadora Duncan, who had a school then, he asked her if she wanted another student. "Bring me the child," she said. Of course, in those days, I was not looking like what I look like today. So she said, "Oh yes, I like him!" But I wasn't very successful as a dancer. I played an angel, but when you're not an angel it's difficile. *I did, however, hear some grand music there. Musicians used to play in her garden, and I remember hearing Debussy's* Afternoon of a Faun *and the music made me feel* the faun.

Grappelli got his first violin when he was twelve, and began to teach himself to play. "I never had a teacher, so I learn good position and posture from sheer luck." He progressed rapidly and was soon able to hold down a gig which would supplement his father's meager income. "At fourteen I got a job in a pit band in a cinema. That's where I really learned to play and to read music, three hours during the day, three in the evening. I played in tune, and that's why they kept me."

It was around this time (1922) that Stephane first heard and played jazz. In an interview with Jan Albert of Pacifica radio station WBAI he says: "The first jazz record I heard on a machine box from America, of course, it was 'Stumbling' by Mitchell's *Jazz Kings*. I was absolutely hypnotized by that kind of music; I used to go every day to listen to the same tune."

Jan Albert: *Where was this phonograph that you listened on?*

Stephane Grappelli: *Near the picturehouse I was working in; it was a little shop with all sorts of gadgets. There was one where you could hear some record with something in your ear—you'd put a coin in. Everyday for one month, two months, maybe as much as a year, I'd listen to the same record.*
So I meet a friend, about my age, who was playing the piano for dancing lessons and he asked me if I can join him for these lessons. So I asked permission to go there. I put someone in my place—I was quite curious. We start to play tango, waltz, one-step, some funny Spanish dance. Then we played fox-trots, "Lady Be Good," "Tea for Two," and all those tunes—that's the first time I played a fox-trot. He offered me the job three times a week, and I preferred to play three times a week than all week at the picture, so I give up my job at the picture to stay there and play "Lady Be Good." (laughter) And I still play "Lady Be Good"—and I'm not fed up with it!

Around 1926 Stephane decided that he wasn't making enough money playing the violin, so he began to accept engagements as a pianist:

SG *I didn't play the violin—I was making my living by the piano. Because I found that with the violin I was not making any money, so I managed to practice the piano a bit and play the piano.*

JA *Where did you play the piano?*

SG *Well, not in the street, it's too heavy to carry that—I played for dancing, in restaurants, things like that. For instance, we'd play dance music when a lady wants to give a party for the first teeth of her baby (laughter). You see, at that time there was no phonograph, no radio, no television, so if you want to listen to some music you must have an orchestra or a pianist—and I was quite busy as a pianist.*

JA *How long was that period when you were making your living as a pianist?*

SG *I played the piano till 1930 or something like that. I was playing with Gregor and the Gregorians and we opened in Nice in 1929. I was one of the pianists because we were two—I remember my old friend Stephane Moujon who I had played with for the dancing lessons—it was the only orchestra where they had two Stephanes on the piano. One day we went to a nightclub and we were all a bit gay, and Gregor said "I heard you used to play the violin." But he insists, he says, "Why don't you play the violin a bit—I've heard that you can play it."—I said, "well,*

I forget." Anyway, he ask about it so much that I was quite curious my-self to see if I still can play. So I borrow a violin from someone in the orchestra and I start to play dance music in the way I feel—Gregor was quite surprised at that and he decided to keep me as a violinist instead of a pianist.

JA *Well, you must have been pretty much out of practice by then?*

SG *Yes, but it's like swimming, it starts quick again.*

JA *Was it unusual for someone to be playing jazz on the violin at that time in Paris?*

SG *Yes. At the beginning when I start to play my own way, people thought I was playing out of tune, because they were used to the strict melody. I was playing the violin in a club in Montparnasse when, one night,* **Django Reinhardt** *came down. He heard I was playing the violin that way and he was quite interested and he asked me if we could do something together.*

Django and Stephane didn't get a chance to play with one another on this occasion, however, and they were to part company for five more years. Stephane took advantage of this time to add another instrument to his arsenal:

After I left Gregor and the Gregorians *I got an engage-ment as a pianist in a small club in the south of France. The woman who ran the club asked me if I could play the saxophone, and of course I lie and say yes. In those days I would do anything to make money: I got one of the five guys from the* Gregorians *to show me where to put my fingers. Now this damn woman asks me for an audition: I remember I played "I Want to Be Happy."* Alors, *you know, you don't need a cen-tury to learn that tune. But, I was unlucky even with that tune, and I played some terrible notes—so I finished up that damn audition by dancing the charleston! You can do those kind of things when you're twenty. Well, she was terribly happy, and I keep on playing the saxo-phone, and I got quite good. A lot of people would hire me to play third alto, which is the most difficult part—very intricate harmony. I played for about five or six years.*

The formation of *The Quintet of the Hot Club of France* came about almost accidentally as Django and Stephane found themselves hired to play in the same dance band, unbeknownst to one another.

Stephane Grappelli: *In 1933, end of '33, we were in the same orchestra, it's one of those coincidences—we were playing at* The Claridge *hotel on the Champs Elysées for the tea dancing—two hours every afternoon, five to seven. During the interval Django used to disappear behind the* *curtain, sit there, alone, with his guitar—and, one day I was playing the violin, and I break a string, so I went behind too and I found him there. While I changed my string we were talking, and like that. . .then when I put my string back and start to tune up, he put some chords behind me and we start to play like that! We loved to play together—we thought it was very amusing so, every interval, we went behind and start to play and one day his brother came, he also play guitar and then it was like a snowball.*

Hughes Panassie decided one day to repeat his little concert we did in a cellar once, but in a better way. He got a small theater, about three hundred seats, and he managed to fill the place. We played, the four of us—Django Reinhardt, his brother, the bass player who was the chef d'orchestre *of the hotel where we were, and me; so, we must find a name for that, because we wanted to be known, and as Panassie formed* The Hot Club of France, *to give him a compliment (because, after all, if we were known to all the musicians in America it was because of him) so, it was a courtesy to call our little group* The Quintet of the Hot Club of France.

Jan Albert: *How long did you play together?*

SG *From 1934 in and out till Django died in 1953.*

JA *When did you make your first recording. . .was that exciting?*

SG *It was terribly exciting because nobody wanted to record us to start. It was a young man named Rauol Caldione who had a small company called Ultrafox—he said, "Well, I'm not terribly interested because jazz music without saxophone, trumpet, drums or piano is not jazz music, but, if it costs me nothing, I will try to make a record." So we were all excited, because we were young—"Oh, we're going to make a record."*
We went there one morning, and Django didn't like that very much at all, because he liked to sleep late. But we were there in the morning because the afternoon was reserved only for stars and well-known people. So we were obliged to go there at nine o'clock. Well, Django arrived at about half past ten after a having a few too many drinks the night before, and he wasn't in a good mood.
In any case, we started to play, and in one set we did "Lady Be Good," "Tiger Rag," "I Saw Stars," and "Sweet Sue"; those were our first four tunes.

JA *Did people buy the records? Did they like them?*

SG *Not only the people, but the company immediately decided to discover us. Soon after, Django and I were recording for every company in Paris!*

The quintet recorded profusely between 1934 and the outbreak of World War II in 1939. Stephane spent the war years in London performing with pianist George Shearing.

Stephane and Django were reunited after the war, but they performed and recorded together with less frequency. Their last recording sessions together took place in Rome during January and February of 1949. The tremendous number of sides produced at these sessions include piano, bass, and drums instead of the stereotypical *Hot Club* guitar sound and feature both Stephane and Django in their most exhilarating moments.

Django died in 1953 of a cerebral hemorrhage while playing billiards. Stephane remained in Reinhardt's shadow for a few years after his death, even though he continued to work steadily.

In the early sixties Grappelli had an engagement playing at the *Paris Hilton,* a job which he was to keep for close to five years. The widespread exposure precipitated an upswing in Stephane's career which has continued unabated up until this present day.

The last ten years Grappelli has recorded and performed as prolifically as any musician in jazz. Albums include pairings with Gary Burton, Oscar Peterson, Yehudi Menuhin, Jean-Luc Ponty, and Joe Pass among many others. Stephane is an indefatigable traveler who keeps up a pace that would wreck a man half his years. As he told Whitney Balliet of the *New Yorker:* . . .*when I'm not working two weeks, I'm* melancolique. *The world stop. And I like different scenery. If I am offer a beautiful contract in the best place for a year I refuse it. I must fold up my blanket and my cot and move on.*

The following interview took place backstage at *The Other End,* a club in Greenwich Village where Grappelli was appearing. I tried to steer away from biographical or historical questions, concentrating instead on musically substantial matters. To begin, I asked Stephane if he had any favorites out of the hundreds of recordings he's made.

GRappelli INTERVIEW

Stephane Grappelli: *I never listen to myself; alors, I can't tell you what I like or what I don't like—it's difficult because I'm never listening—I'm not curious, you see. I like to hear somebody else, but not me, because it's quite enough when I'm playing, why shall I listen to me when I'm not playing! But, I like to hear some other people—that gives me great pleasure—I like to play, but not hearing myself all the time. I never practice because I can't stand it.*

Matt Glaser: *So for you, the moment when you're playing is the important thing.*

SG *That's right—the moment. It all depends on what people I've got in front of me and behind me. It's like a hair, you see? Very thin—you start well or you don't start well, you know what I mean? When you are lucky you are lucky, and when you are not lucky you are not lucky.*
I like to play, but I don't like to practice. I never open my violin case when I'm in a room by myself. I can't stand it. When we practice some arrangement I'm willing to do that—play for hours, if necessary, but not by myself.

MG *Was this always the case, or did you practice when you were young?*

SG *No, I've always been like that, all my life. When my father gave me that small violin, three-quarter size, when I was twelve years old, I was quite curious in the beginning, like all children. But I did not suffer too much with it—some children don't like it when you give them a violin to play, but as I liked music so much, I tried to make some sound come out of that damn violin, like I used to do on the piano, see? But, I never practice, and when I was about fourteen, I was obliged to make some money, because we were poor. My father was original and intelligent; the only intelligence he missed was the intelligence to make money—he couldn't do it. So one day we were so poor, and I saw some people playing in the courtyard. In Paris all the houses are at least six floors and they have a courtyard so a lot of musicians used to play at that time, without radio, without TV, without gramophone. So they used to go to the courtyards and the people would open their window and throw money in a little piece of newspaper or cloth. I saw those people doing that I said, "Why not me?" and so I started doing that and playing the violin like that.*

MG *How did you learn to play without a teacher?*

SG *Well, I'm not alone—like Django Reinhardt, Errol Garner, Art Tatum—I don't think they had a teacher in their life—we just play,* *that's all. Of course, the more and more you play, the more you make progress. I remember, before the war, we used to play from ten o'clock to six o'clock in the morning in those clubs in Paris—ten to six—no stop. When we had good customers we'd stay till eight or ten; they'd drink a lot of champagne and give us a lot of money, so of course we were obliged to stay. That's how I learned to play, by playing a long time, long time, long time!*

MG *When you were younger you studied solfège?*

SG *That's the only thing I learn in my life—solfège—because of my father. My father was a teacher, so at least he knew that; he said, "If you want to play the violin or the piano the best thing to do to learn quick is to study solfège and to learn to read music." So he showed me how to read music—he showed me where was C, A, A flat and I learned to read quite fast. I was lucky.*

MG *Were you able to apply your knowledge of the piano to the violin in some way?*

SG *I think so. When you've got a good ear you can apply its harmonic aspect. I like the piano more than the violin; you sit down when you play. The violin is just my gimmick.*

MG *When did you first meet Eddie South?*

SG *Well, Eddie South arrived in Paris in 1937 for the Paris Exhibition at the time; he was playing there. And, of course, some people asked if we would perform together and we did that along with another violinist, Michel Warlop—three violins. That's how I meet him—a nice person, a gentleman and a divine musician—Hugues Panassie used to call him "The Black Angel." We played, he left Paris and I never saw him again. His playing was so perfect, like Joe Venuti—he's another one who had such a fabulous sound. I think I could recognize the sound of Joe Venuti. But of Eddie South, the only work of his I know is the record he made with us.*

MG *How did that recording of the Bach "Double Violin Concerto" come about?*

SG *It was the idea of Charles Delaunay, and of course, I was against that, because I was the only one who could read music, you see. Eddie could read music, but not so well—he did his best because he had such a warm tone and all that, but Django was completely lost in the piano part—it's very tricky, you see—you can't accompany that like a Neapolitan melody—it's serious music—intricate. I saw the piano part; it is quite difficult to play and when you do straight rhythm it is not good enough. So in my opinion we should leave Bach alone and play some jazz tune instead. But apparently some masochists like it—so there you are. I don't know, as long as they like it. But to me I don't think it was very serious to do that—it was Mr. Charles Delaunay's idea. When you hear Menuhin and Oistrakh play that with a pianist who can really play the part on the harpsichord, for instance, that sounds different. I think it's a danger to jazz some classical music—it's a mistake. It's like when I hear on the* *radio the fifth symphony of Beethoven in disco—well, they should be in jail, those guys—*

MG   (Laughter)

SG   *I'm sorry, I mean it. It's disgusting. I think we have enough jazz tunes, we can compose some more—we have enough tunes to leave classical music alone.*

MG   *But classical music does have an influence on jazz. . . .*

SG   *When you play jazz, of course you have some reminiscence, like Art Tatum, Debussy and Ravel, and modern—Bartok sometimes. Because in jazz music you've got all sorts of music—all the music is in jazz—rhythm, swing, melody, ad libitum—everything—ballad—there is everything. And the fantastic thing is, in jazz, you can play a tune slow, fast, medium—everything. You can't give treatment like that to a concerto of Beethoven. It's nearly mechanical now, the classical, because you must play, for the purists, absolutely perfect with the correct tempo and all that. There is no fantasy, you see what I mean; in fact, it's a beautiful thing to hear, but there is no fantasy. In jazz, you can do what you want, which is marvelous. In jazz you are a composer, because you are an improviser; an improviser is a composer.*

MG   *What do you do when you run into a wall while you're improvising?*

SG   *It's like what I told you before; you must start well. Sometimes you miss a break, for instance. If you miss the first note, it's harrowing; you lose contact, you lose everything. That's the difficult part in jazz music; technically, jazz is not difficult, if you know your instrument well. In jazz, you do your improvisation, but you do what you can do; in classical music, you must do what you can't do, which is quite different; Suppose I am working on a concerto on the violin or the piano; I am absolutely obliged to play what is written, I can't change the chord. But in jazz, you can. You play the chord, you can do, what is your possibilité. That's why there is so much range of artist—bad, mediocre, medium, good, very good, and genius. Look—Oscar Peterson, Errol Garner, George Shearing the way they play the piano—well, I can't compare them with Horowitz, they play another kind of music—*

MG   *Horowitz loved Art Tatum, I've heard some stories—*

SG   *Because those people are great artists, great technicians and they've got a lot of inspiration.*

MG   *What happens to you on an evening if you don't feel particularly inspired?*

SG   *Oh, that's a difficult thing; but it is quite interesting. I love to play; if I've got a good accompaniment, I'm okay immediately. I like to have a glass of Scotch, of course, before I go on the stage to put my metabolism in good order. Scotch whiskey is a help, a kind of medicine for me—then, good musicians, good company, and that's enough for me to im-*

provise. *I can't improvise if I see a musician and I can't feel immediately if they are enthusiastic or not. That's the main thing—my accompanists—if I feel they are not enthusiastic, it is not worth it, to play. But I'm lucky. I've always been, and I think I've got a kind of flair for that, I always play with good artists. Not only are they good, but they love what they do, and they appreciate other people, which is such a great help.*

MG *When you're improvising, do you hear exactly what you're going to do next, do you have a general idea, or is it in your hands?*

SG *I know very well what you mean. You see, it is a question of luck. Sometimes you have a good inspiration—not even thinking what you are doing! I've noticed, that's why I like to escape with a little drink, not too much of course, good musicians, good faces near me, good public, and I've noticed—you play better when you are not thinking of what you're doing! Suppose, when I'm playing an important concert—you know—Carnegie Hall, Albert Hall in London, or a command performance for the Queen of England—*

MG *Have you done that?*

SG *Yes, of course.* (laughter) *But,* alors, *then I know I will have a break there—you know, those two bars—*alors*—the band stops for two bars—the break. Of course, I want to prepare something; while I'm playing I'm thinking what I'm going to do for those two bars, and* inevitably *it's not good—but I always get back on my feet. But if I'm not thinking of that, it's always good. When you think to do something, you make a mistake. Improvisation is not an effort, it is just something natural to me. Improvisation is. . .you can do it; if you can't do it, you can't do it, but if you can do it, it's not an effort.*
Suppose the solo violinist with the Berlin Philharmonic is in front of me, he makes me nervous, that guy. So, it's an effort for me to escape from his vision; and, I must shut my eyes and think of something else. Then I go on with success.

MG *Did playing with Menuhin make you nervous?*

SG *Not at all. Because he's an easy man, and he's a great artist. You know, when you are playing with a musician, because Menuhin has never been in the front of me when I'm playing—he travels so much he has no time to go and see some people, but we record together and do some television shows, we are working together, so we are not afraid together. It's when you see some musician in the front of you—like I was told that when Art Tatum would go where Oscar Peterson was performing, Oscar would get nervous, I can't believe it, but maybe thirty years ago it could be. The sight of a great name in music—it makes you nervous. When you know that Michel Legrand is in the front of you, you say, "Oh my God, I must be careful tonight." But when you are careful, that's when you don't play well!*

MG *Can you remember any instances in your life when you felt you could do anything on the violin that you wanted to do?*

SG *I would like to do some impossible things, but I don't want to in-*

vestigate too much when I'm working. I never prepare anything at home because I'm incapable of inventing anything at home. I can't prepare a coda or an introduction or anything like that—I can't. I must do that on the spot, when I hear the chord. Alone, I'm incapable of preparing something. Of course, sometimes I'm thinking of something, but when I take my violin out and say, "I'd like to try that," I can't, because I forget.

I'm so used to improvising now that I don't like to read music. Suppose one of my colleagues would like to play something, I say, "Okay, play that for me," and I'm very lazy, I don't want to learn that by ear, it's too long. So I take a piece of paper and I have my friend or colleague play that and I put that on the paper. Then, I read that and I learn the tune—and it's quicker for me. Sometimes, if you've got a difficult rhythm, or difficult passage—it's very hard to learn by ear. If I didn't read music, like Django, I would maybe learn that quicker, but now that I'm so used to reading music I'm not as quick as I used to be.

MG   *Did you learn most standards by ear?*

SG   *Oh yes. You see, when you start young (and I started when I was fourteen) it's like when you learn a language. If I learned English when I was fourteen I'm sure I'd speak it better than now, when I start to learn when I was thirty-two—music is the same. You learn quicker when you are before sixteen; after that, it's more difficult.*

MG   *Can you trace how your playing has changed over the years?*

SG   *I don't think I've changed. I'm incapable. . .even if I play "Nuages," now I play that for twenty-five years, I never do the same coda every night—never. Sometimes I'm in a good mood, I do it well, sometimes mediocre. Of course, because of the respect I have for the public, I always manage to finish up as well as I possibly can. But sometimes, when I've got real inspiration and I'm not thinking of what I'm doing, it goes well.*

But I don't think I've changed my style at all. I change because I never can repeat what I've done. I can't improvise on a tune or a melody twice the same way—it's impossible. I've got some start and some finishing, because I must be disciplined with the boys who play with me; if we decide to finish on such a chord, I must do it—that's the only thing I do all the time. But true inspiration, true improvisation, can never be the same. It's not new, improvisation—it's always existed—look at the partitas of Bach—a theme with variations. The caprices of Paganini are one theme with twenty-four improvisations—jazz is the same. After all, Chopin used to improvise, Beethoven improvised, all great artists improvise. It's a shame there was no machine to record an improvisation of Beethoven.

MG   *But over the years, you've expanded your style. . .*

SG   *I know what you mean. The world of music expands also; now you've got the rock, the pop—you've got a lot of things like that with a new sound which opened a lot of doors for me. Without immersing myself too much in the world of pop, I must admit that there is some fantastic work in it. I can't play that music because I am not playing electric; I leave that to my good friend Jean-Luc Ponty—he's a master of that. In spite of me, I'm obliged to accept the new sound. I have young* *musicians with me; John Ethridge, a guitarist who used to play pop, he's a pop player and jazz as well, and Brian Torff, a twenty-four year old. They are born with the pop music, and they influence me a lot, you see. So, in spite of me, I've investigated a little bit of the world which was unknown to me ten years ago.*

MG   *When did you first meet Jean-Luc Ponty?*

SG   *He came to see me in my place in Paris when I used to live in Montmartre. He was very young; I think he was seventeen or eighteen. He introduced himself, and I was very pleased to know him because I realized immediately that he had the possibility to do something; well, I couldn't guess at that time, fifteen years ago, how he would play today. When he told me he'd won first prize at the Paris Conservatory and was playing first violin in the symphony orchestra in Paris every Sunday, I get, of course, terribly interested. I said, "Well, he's not one of those stupid young musicians who wants advice or wants to see me for what reason I don't know. He has an enormous talent with him already."*
So we meet like that. He managed to come several times, and we used to play the double concerto of Bach, for practicing. I didn't mind to do it, because somebody else was with me. I will never practice that alone, but with him, I did, and I was terribly interested because that made me practice. I remember we used to call that piece "The Bible." We'd say, "Now we're going to do 'The Bible'." He'd bring his violin and, of course, to be able to play together we'd play the Bach "Double" and repeat, repeat, repeat.
I have great affection for that boy because he's an intelligent person apart from being a very good violinist and he proved he was intelligent because he really, in my opinion, invented something on the violin. And I'm proud of him, because we all invented something; Joe (Venuti), maybe myself too, we did something else which was different in those days. And now Jean-Luc too. There is a young violinist in Paris named Didier Lockwood; well, he still has a shell on his back, but one day he'll get rid of that shell and really produce something. He's between Jean-Luc and everybody else. He's twenty-one and he came to see me like all of them do, and I feel he's going in a certain direction which will be something really quite different from everything else in the modern style.
Life and art is an eternal innovation; it's always changing. What is the best style? Nobody knows. But it changes all the time.

MG   *You inspire all these people to do something on the violin in a new way; to young violinists there's something so magical about improvising on the violin and you're the person they associate with that magical feeling—how do you feel about this?*

SG   *I feel, in my position, all right because I'm glad there are people who've invented something—like Jean-Luc or Didier or Venuti himself, the way he used to play in the beginning, sixty years ago.*
It's exactly like (Louis) Armstrong; till the end of his life he used to play the same, he never changed his style. Because his style was so established, he doesn't need to change—he's a genius. Alors, after him was (Dizzy) Gillespie, another extraordinary player; but Armstrong didn't worry about Gillespie, you see what I mean? It was no necessity for Armstrong to change his style, because his style was so perfect. Alors, me, my posi-

tion is a bit like that with Jean-Luc Ponty; I'm very glad Jean-Luc plays like that, which is a continuation of all what we did before him. Like Stuff Smith has a great place in the jazz music too. Stuff really invented swing on the violin; we all swing, mind you, but his aggressivité is very agreeable. It's very aggressive violin playing. Not very gentle, but it swings like crazy.

My style has changed with my hair. Someone once said, "You gain in artistry as you lose your hair." I don't know if I prefer to have my hair or my artistry!

Everyone tries to perfect themselves, to do better and better. I try and perfect my sound, my technique to please people who listen. But I don't want to play too much. When you improvise, it's like having an appetite, if you eat too much, you lose your appetite, but if you don't play too much, you like to play.

STEPHANE'S STYLE

Stephane Grappelli

Stephane Grappelli's violin style is a remarkable and complex phenomenon. Without formal training of any kind he was able to develop a technique of staggering fluidity and, simultaneously, an improvisational approach which is totally unique. Let's begin our analysis of his style with a closer look at the physical components of his technique.

"I play my own style—I bought it myself from my body."

Stephane learned to play the violin by watching and listening—watching others and listening to his own inner ear. He'd been blessed with prodigious mind-to-hand coordination as is amply evidenced by both his piano and violin techniques.

In mastering the violin, Stephane has always taken the path of least resistance and plays the way which is most natural for his body (hence the quote above). Conservation of energy and a minimum amount of motion are the rules here. Stephane is completely relaxed when he plays—not the slightest physical strain. That's why, at the age of seventy-two, Stephane's playing it at it's peak, whereas most classical violinists at that age have long since begun to deteriorate and lose muscular control. (Violin pedagogue Kato Havas cites Grappelli's technique as an example of a perfectly integrated and natural approach to the instrument.) Stephane told Don Bacon of *Coda Magazine* that playing jazz on the violin is not difficult. "Nothing is difficult when you can do it. The only difficulty at my age is to stand up for long periods at a time." I think this gives us some idea of the organic nature of Grappelli's technique.

bowinc

I learned mostly by watching classical violinists. I think it's important to hold the bow in the classical manner. The bow should always follow the left hand, and give accentuation to key notes. It's good to end a phrase on a down bow.

Stephane plays the rapid eighth-notes which make up such a large part of his musical vocabulary near the tip of the bow, somewhere between the top of the third and bottom of the fourth quarter. This very precise back-and-forth motion seems to come from the lower forearm, with the wrist remaining straight. Stephane's bow hold is very gentle, and relaxed; his fingers appear to do no more than rest on the frog.

Even at full throttle on an up tempo tune Stephane still uses very small bow strokes. His bow is generally placed closer to the fingerboard than to the bridge, and it rarely leaves the string. A partial explanation for his amazingly adept bowing can be found in an aforementioned quote where he says, "The bow should always follow the left hand." Stephane seems to treat the bow as a servant and executor of his musical idea, as opposed to an exteriorized element.

One time, shortly after I first met him, I asked Mr. Grappelli for some remarks about bowing. He spent a few minutes entertaining me with some scintillating passages and then said simply, "The bow must go up and down." Far from being meaningless, this Zen koan-like statement gets right to the heart of the matter; all that the bow *can* do is go up and down! Moreover, Grappelli's answer indicated the total absence of artifice in his approach to making music on the violin.

Left Hand

The concertmaster of a major American symphony has remarked that Stephane Grappelli plays with purer intonation than many concert artists before the public today. One reason for this, apart from Stephane's impeccable ears, is his sparing use of vibrato. "Some notes should have no vibrato, blue notes for instance." Stephane uses vibrato as an expressive device to add color, but certainly not on every note. His vibrato is extremely fast and focused; it originates in his hand.

Stephane keeps his fingers in a gentle curve. He comes into notes almost parallel to the string, as opposed to hitting them from above. This minute slide into each note lands him on the fleshiest part of his finger, which is one of the factors responsible for his clear, rich tone. Very light finger pressure is another Grappelli trademark; just enough to get the job done, no bearing down unnecessarily on notes. This allows Stephane to play at incredibly fast tempos. Don Bacon of *Coda Magazine* has remarked, "Watching and listening to him play at tempi that would test the mind and strength of Elvin Jones is an audio-visual experience of unparalleled intensity, such is the agility of his mind and body."

improvisational style

Stephane's miraculous violin technique is a reflection of his basic aesthetic, or world-view, elements of which include elegance, ease, charm, grace, and beauty. "All my life I've liked the good things. I don't like ordinary things. I've always valued *élégance* and beauty. I'll leave it to others to describe that word *élégance*. It is not for me to say if I'm *élégant* or not."

Far from being something amorphous, these ideals can be said to be the direct progenitor of Grappelli's improvisational style and, subsequently, of his violin technique. To understand this hierarchical relationship better, we can look at the connection between speech and improvised music. In both cases, the idea being expressed is the primary thing. Next would come a language adequate to express the idea, and in music this would correspond to the performer's own vocabulary. (This is the level of Grappelli's style which we're about to examine.) Finally, we come to the purely technical level; in speech, this corresponds to grammar, syntax, morphology; in music, the physical technique of the performer.

Stephane's improvisational style can be recognized as far back as the first recordings he made with Django in 1934. Like all great improvisers, Grappelli has remained true to his original conception. He has, of course, expanded, deepened, and polished his style, but, as he says, "I don't think I've changed my style at all. I change (only) because I never can repeat what I've done. I can't improvise on a tune twice the same way—it's impossible."

Stephane is, and has always been, a melodic player:

I think it's better that when you start to play, play strictly melody. Everybody should, by politeness to the composer, play what he composed! I got that idea from Benny Goodman when I was twenty-two, twenty-three. I was amazed with his quality you see, with Gene Krupa, Lionel Hampton, marvelous, also Teddy Wilson with whom I have had the pleasure to play with not so long ago. A marvelous pianist. He was in fact the favorite pianist of Django. So all these records gave me the idea, because I was in such a hurry to improvise on anything, why not first expose nicely the theme?

. . .So if I play the melody first, the audience knows later on what I'm doing; it's based on that melody but it's absolutely something else. I like to expose the theme, but after I play the theme I like to go somewhere else myself. I play often with my eyes shut so I can't see anybody, because I want to escape the people that are in front of me. But I like at the same time feeling their presence. Jazz playing comes naturally. I just put my finger anywhere and be very attentive to what I've got behind me. If the accompaniment is absolutely perfect and I know they are going to do a certain chord, in the right moment then I can launch myself in an arabesque and what you call improvisation, which is in fact improvisation on a theme. You try to find a melodic line. That means you and the composer get very close, alike. The musician takes only the chords and (it is true, no?) does something absolutely different.

Stephane, like any jazz musician worth his salt, cites Louis Armstrong as a major influence. When he was eighteen he heard an Armstrong recording and, as he says, "that changed my destiny." Other early influences included Bix Beiderbecke's piano playing, Red Nichols, Duke Ellington, Coleman Hawkins, Benny Carter, and, of paramount importance, Art Tatum.

As a matter of fact, I don't think my music is based on a violinistic style. Art Tatum gave me ideas. A lot of people ask me if I had inspiration. Somewhere of course, somebody is always before you, like your father. I always listened to other instruments; the saxophone, the clarinet—Benny Goodman, Artie Shaw, Woody Herman, but I never listened much to a single violinist. There were no jazz violinists at all, or only one—Joe Venuti, who I admired intensely, but at the time, I was not considering his music as real jazz. Jazz grew to be a new style; a mixture of Debussy and Ravel, as a matter of fact, is what all the best jazzmen based their music upon.

This last sentence displays a little bit of Stephane's justifiable French chauvanism, and his style is nothing if not French. The Gallic elements of Grappelli's style include a penchant for rubato and an impressionistic use of tone color. Stephane's first instrument was the piano (on which he is still an amazing virtuoso) and he has been successful in transferring some of the keyboard's inherent impressionism to the violin. Strangely enough, we can thank Art Tatum for the fact that Stephane Grappelli is primarily a violinist, "I heard him on record for the first time in 1935, and was so astonished and disturbed by his genius that I temporarily lost my enthusiasm for the piano and determined to concentrate on the violin."

Guitarist Ike Isaacs, an associate of Grappelli's for many years, has remarked, "Stephane is really a pianist on the violin because he thinks both vertically and horizontally. He has a wonderfully receptive mind, musically. When I play passages with him 'colla voce', he responds instantly to chord variations. He has a great harmonic sense and very acute ears."

As Isaacs pointed out, Stephane is very responsive to the musicians with him:

It all depends on the musicians that I'm playing with. If I'm playing with Martial Solal I won't play in the same style as with Oscar Peterson. The water goes where there is a possibility for it to go— music is the same. When I play with people who are playing in Django's style, instinctively, I go back to the way I played years ago. And if I was to play with McCoy Tyner, I'm sure that marvelous musician would make me play differently than I do now.

MUSICAL LANGUAGE

Stephane uses primarily diatonic scales when he improvises. He rarely uses jazz scales (such as diminished, whole-tone or modal) per se, although he certainly has absorbed a substantial amount of bebop phrasing.

Stephane, like many great improvisers, has a tremendous stockpile of melodic motifs, (most about two bars in length) that he is able to mold and alter to fit any given musical situation (See table on next page.)

Here I've extracted about twenty of Grappelli's most commonly used phrases as they occur in the transcriptions. These motifs can be conveniently organized into five basic categories.

A TABLE OF STEPHANE GRAPPELLI'S MELODIC MOTIFS

Class 1 Descending phrases with strong emphasis on the sixth and ninth degree of the scale. Distinctly Grappelli-esque, these motifs appear frequently in the transcriptions.

CLASS 1

Class 2 Jagged and angular licks, often based on a particularly violinistic capability. Stephane uses these ear-catching phrases when the heat is fierce.

CLASS 2

Class 3   *Modular* patterns, usually based on arpeggio's; Stephane plays them most often in descending form. With their own inner logic, these types of patterns can be used ad infinitum. Grappelli, however uses them in a discreet manner.

CLASS 3

3A

3B

3C

Class 4   Assorted and sundry *jazzy* licks. Common devices here include chromatic tones, flatted fifths, diminished arpeggios, and bluesy phrases.

CLASS 4

4A

4B

4C

Class 5 All motifs with a highly rhythmic quality. Stephane is particularly fond of using strings of repeating triplets. Also common is the insistent, trumpet-like, hammer-on lick.

CLASS 5

5A

5B

5C

5D

5E

      All the motifs, as they appear in the transcriptions, have been isolated and listed. In the analysis of each tune, there is a list of the type (2B, for instance) of motif and where it appears in that particular transcription. Keep in mind that these motifs may begin at different intervals than notated and that they may only be fragments of the motif which is listed, but nonetheless, they are integrally related.

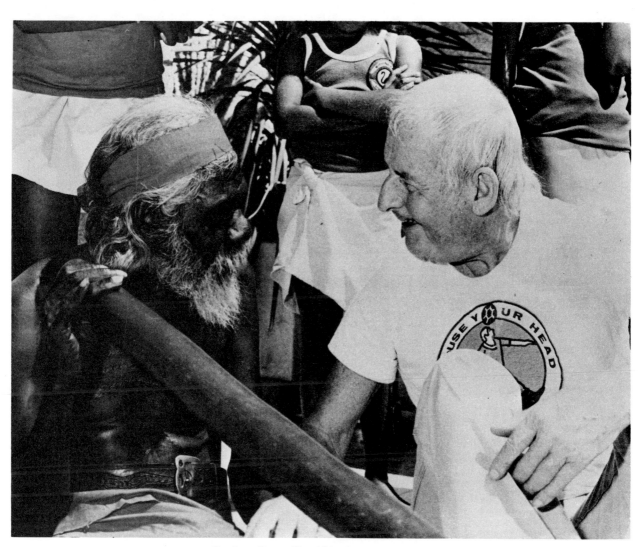

Stephane Grappelli and friend.

READING A TRANSCRIPTION

A transcription of an improvised solo is very different from composed music. Any improvising artist, makes use of the full spectrum of his instrument's capabilities, including many sounds for which there is no notation available. Therefore, the transcriber must devise symbols to indicate the various effects which the player uses (see the table below).

These symbols are useful up to a point, for one may eventually run into the "accuracy vs. readability" problem. I have seen transcriptions which were devilishly accurate, but were not playable because of their complexity. The idea here is to head in the direction of "readability" rather than accuracy. These transcriptions should be used in conjunction with recordings as an aid to learning and not as an end in themselves.

The transcriptions can be most valuable if used in this manner; first, listen to the break a couple of times until you have a good idea of it's structure. Then, listen to it again and follow along with the transcription. Do this a number of times, so that your ear may comprehend the more difficult passages. Finally, take out the fiddle and play through the transcription *very slowly*. Hopefully, this process will help you absorb some elements of the player's style which can not be transmitted through a transcription (tone, articulation, stress, and other crucial aspects of phrasing).

All eighth notes, unless otherwise indicated, should be played with a swing feel.

Bowings are based on whatever I could glean from recordings, combined with hours of watching Stephane closely. I can't claim that they are totally accurate, but they should help give you the proper feeling.

Let's begin to examine the styles of our six violinists. What we have here are two choruses of the blues by each man, transcribed from various recordings and placed on a large staff. (I'm indebted to John Mehegan's incredible book *Jazz Rhythm and the Improvised Line* published by Amsco Music Publishing Company for this idea.) This approach enables us to compare each player's use of melodic rhythm, and to see, at a glance, how they shape their phrases.

1   **Eddie South** ("Eddie's Blues" — *Djangologie #5* EMI Pathe CO54-16005). A good example of Eddie's deliberate, almost operatic style. Notice the large, ravishing phrases and the slightly romantic rubato. Absence of blue notes, sparing use of slides. Covers most of fingerboard.

2   **Joe Venuti** ("Blues for Nobody" — *Joe Venuti in Milan* Durium msA 77277). Highly declamatory, strong, almost mean. Heavy triplet feel, many slides into flatted third, flatted seventh. Joe often used arpeggios, especially major seventh ones. Eighth-note passages often lead to long, sustained notes in the higher register, reminiscent of some clarinet players. Powerful detaché bowing, knowledgable use of double stops.

3   **Stephane Grappelli** ("Blues in the Dungeon" — *Stuff Smith* Everest FS 238). It's interesting to note that Stephane has recorded duo albums with all of the violinists under discussion. Both Stephane and Stuff's two choruses come from this valuable Everest reissue.

Stephane begins his first chorus with an elegant, highly melodic statement in the best "story-telling" jazz tradition. He gradually increases rhythmic movement and melodic embellishment while continuing to keep up a pretty consistent use of slides and blue notes. The second chorus begins with an intense *falling-down-stairs* riff which illustrates Stephane's debt to Eddie South. High position work and emphasis on the flat-five lead into a forceful ending, employing parallel fifths.

4   **Stuff Smith** ("Blues in the Dungeon" — *Stuff Smith* Everest FS 238).

The most important aspects of Stuff's style cannot be illustrated adequately through music notation. You can't illustrate his incredible sense of swing, hoarse tone, wide vibrato, subtle phrasing, and unique, jazz, expressive intonation. Since his playing consisted mostly of these ineffable characteristics, I've not devoted very much time to him in this book, although he certainly was one of the giants of jazz violin.

Stuff spoke the blues language most convincingly, and his two choruses employ spills, slides, and anything else that could help him achieve a gutteral, human sound. Stuff's message comes not so much through the harmonic substance of the break (he slides into the flatted-third thirty-nine times by my count) as through it's powerful rhythmic content. All eighth-notes should be swung heavily.

5   **Svend Asmussen** ("Timme's Blues" — *Violin Summit* MPS 5C 064 61227)

This has always been one of my favorite improvised violin solos. The placement of accents and stress points in the first chorus are so odd that I often think the rhythm section and Svend are in two different places.

Asmussen plays in a manner dictated by his aesthetic, compositional bent, not so much by violinistic considerations. He has an obvious command of bop vocabulary, and his bowing has a strong horn-like inflection. Svend plays with a sophisticated over-the-bar-line feeling. Notice how he waits a measure before beginning his solo and extends it by two bars at the end. This break is not a very demanding one technically, but it's extremely satisfying musically!

6   **Jean-Luc Ponty** ("Sniffin' the Blues" — *Les Grandes Violiniste de Jazz* Philips 6612 039).

Ponty, in these two searing choruses, demonstrates his complete control of the harmonic material in modern jazz. He has made a successful transference of bop and post-bop (Coltrane) language to the violin. He uses the higher, extension intervals of the chord (7, 9,

11, 13) and many implied passing chords, including altered ii-V7-I patterns. The solo contains a tremendous amount of activity, both rhythmically and texturally; held notes turn into double-time passages which then give way to earthier, bluesy phrases in weird double-stops.

Ponty's sound here is Miles Davis inspired—dry, acerbic, with no vibrato. His immaculate control of the bow doesn't falter, even in the midst of ultra-sophisticated compound rhythms.

Eddie South

Stuff Smith

NOTATIONAL symbols

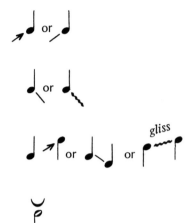

Slide—
slide into note from slightly below pitch.

Fall off or **spill—**
slide down from note to indistinct pitch.
(can also be used as a "fall up":

Glissando or **gliss—**
slide, up or down, from one to another.

Bend—
a slight dip in pitch immediately followed
by a return to the original pitch; a "da-
oo-wah" sound.

Ghost(ed) or **swallowed note—**
a note with rhythmic value but an implied rather than definite pitch.

Sag—
raise, or lower, pitch to the general
vicinity indicated by the ghost note.

Trill—
a rapid alternation between the written
note and the pitch above. The upper note
is the next scalewise tone unless otherwise indicated by an accidental or a note
head in parentheses.

Shake—
wide, hysterical vibrato.

Note should sound quarter-tone above
or below pitch indicated.

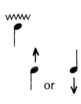

Passage indicated is just a general approximation and should be approached
with caution.

Left-hand pizzicato.

analysis of six jazz violinists

it don't

MEAN A THING
(if it ain't got that swing)

Excuse this ludicrous scenario, but if I were being relegated to a desert island where there was a stereo system, and could take only one jazz violin record with me, I would without hesitation choose *Violin Summit*. This album is the chronicle of a concert which took place in Basel, Switzerland on September 30, 1966, with the participation of Stephane Grappelli, Svend Asmussen, Jean-Luc Ponty, and Stuff Smith. (For more information about the genesis of this recording, see the Ponty interview page 120).

Each one of the fiddlers has a chance to blow on this familiar Ellington tune, and it's a perfect opportunity to compare their styles. Stephane, being the elder statesman of the group, comes up first. His two bird-like choruses capture the excitement which he, and all the other violinists, were experiencing. Grappelli uses motifs 5D(measures 19-20 and 25-26), 2B (measure 35), and 3B (measures 52-54).

Steph passes the baton to Svend, who plays two choruses that amply demonstrate his mastery of swinging, bopish, mainstream jazz. Svend's lines are highly syncopated, horn-like and deeply satisfying, from a jazz point of view. His technique is so good and very much appropriate to the style that you're not aware of this being "violin" jazz, but rather jazz which happens to be played on a violin.

Wheareas Grappelli's tone is light, airy, and fluid, Svend's sound is reedier and more rugged. His bowing has the bite and rhythmic acuity of Stuff Smith combined with the ability to swing even the most harmonically, thorny passages. In contrast to Grappelli's rivers of flowing eighth-notes, Svend will often grab on to one note and toy around with it rhythmically as in measures 97-100 and 107-110. A similar device is used in measures 121-123, where Asmussen, in the best Sonny Rollins fashion, latches on to the suspended fourth, C natural, and punches at it from different angles.

Next up to bat is the young Jean-Luc Ponty, only twenty-four at the time of this recording. Ponty has said that he felt this was an opportunity "to burn," to show his elder colleagues what he was capable of doing. Well, "burn" he most certainly does! For my money, this is the most terrifying and intense acoustic jazz violin solo ever captured on wax. The manifold factors which make this break so exciting include Ponty's total and ravishing technical control of the fiddle, his complete absorption of late bop and early Coltrane language, and his own palpable agitation.

Before we proceed any further, I should point out that there are a number of places here where Ponty employs the John Coltrane *sheets of sound* technique, a wild flurry of notes used more as a gesture—for effect rather than for any specific musical content. I've indicated these measures by bracketing them with dark lines; in some cases I've extrapolated a phrase which is sonically similar to what Ponty plays, but most of the time I've just indicated the general pitch area that he covers. In all of these cases, however, the dark black lines mean, to paraphrase marathon Coltrane transcriber, Andrew White, "watch out!—things get hairy!"

Ponty, although he had only been playing jazz for four or five years at this time, had completely revamped his violin technique to accommodate his jazz ideas. He abandoned the use of vibrato altogether and began to play with a dark tone, all steel and ice, which was the violinistic equivalent of the *hard* Coltrane saxophone sound.

There are a number of detectable influences on Ponty's improvisational style. The most evident ones are bebop, Coltrane, power rock, and contemporary classical. The bebop influence manifests itself most strongly in measures 141-153 and again in measures 177-191, where Ponty employs flat-nine arpeggios, superimposed ii-V-I patterns, and generally stresses the higher intervals of the chords. In measure 198 he plays a descending diminished scale, which is another favorite bebop device.

Besides the periodic *sheets of sound*, Coltrane's influence can be heard in the unrelenting intensity, both rhythmically and structurally, of this break. A rock feeling is imparted through the use of power licks such as the series in chromatically ascending triplets in measures 192-196 and again in measures 205-209.

Ponty himself has suggested that he was influenced by modern classical composition in both his improvising and his composing. It's most evident here in the form of repeating rhythmic motifs. These phrases generally stay on one pitch and they are all three beats long; a simplified synthesis would yield this figure.

Interest is generated as these three-beat figures move through the four-beat bars and the emphasis shifts—

Ponty begins his break with this device (measures 135-140) and subsequently employs it in two other places (measures 200-205 and 209-212). Similar, but less archetypal forms of the same idea are found in measures 153-157, 169-171, and 185-186.

it don't mean a thing i
(if it ain't got that swing)

Violin Summit EMI MPS 5C 064 61227 (import)

Duke Ellington

oh, lady be good 1

Here we have three-and-a-half breaks on this peren-
nial swing favorite. The first two (Grappelli and South) are from a classic 1936 recording in which three violins (Michel Warlop is the third)
play the melody and trade breaks. Stephane begins his break as smooth
as silk and very relaxed. Although harmonically simple, a G blues scale
with periodic chromatic alternations through most of the break, this solo
has an implacable sense of logic and line which makes it a classic.

Grappelli creates great thrust and momentum here
by anticipating chord changes and improvising off of the new chord before it is actually played. This is especially noticeable in measures 16, 20,
and 24.

Stephane doesn't belabor the alarming chromatic
passage in measures 7 and 8. He tosses it off rather lightly, making it
clear that his destination is to the open D on which the phrase ends.

The nifty seventh-laden phrase in measures 21 and
22 has become a staple in any hot bluegrass fiddler's bag of tricks. Another effect here which has been absorbed by country fiddlers is the
"hysterical" vibrato which Stephane uses on the high D in measure 27.

In direct contract to Stephane's continually mov-
ing eighth notes, Eddie South enters with a restrained, secure, and powerful break. His disjunct sense of rhythm gives this break a recitative-like
quality. Standard "South-ern" devices which are employed here include
parallel fifths, descending quintuple phrases, a healthy dose of rubato,
and a biting attack with the bow.

Motifs
1A meas. 16
1B meas. 23-4, 29-31

oh, lady be good 1

Djangologie # 5   EMI PATHE CO54 16005

George Gershwin

SOUTH

OH, lady be good II

Finally, we come to one of Stephane's modern versions of the tune, this one from the delightful Angel recording *Jalousie—Music of the Thirties*, with Yehudi Menuhin.

Stephane's four-bar break takes us from the key of D, (in which the violinists have been playing the melody as a ballad) to G, the standard key for this tune. (Notice the nice octave displacement in the first two bars.)

After a lovely reading of the head, Grappelli executes a triplet-laden, two-bar break (measure 31) signaling a rise in the temperature. He vaults into his solo with a chromatic, boppish lick in third position. Over a subsequent A minor seventh chord he plays an outside variant of motif 2C (measure 41) which ties into a more conservative phrase over a D seventh.

Menuhin plays a Haydn-esque bridge while Grappelli reenters with a trill and a funky, upper-neighbor, arpeggiated figure. After an unexpected detour to E seventh, Stephane takes it out on a variant of motif 1B in the last measure.

Motifs
1B 3rd bar of pick-up
4A 3rd and 4th bar of pick-up;
      33,44
5A meas. 31
3C meas. 57-8

OH, lady be good II

Jalousie—Music of the Thirties ANGEL SFO 36968

George Gershwin

56

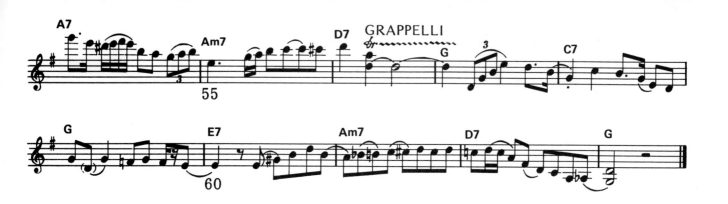

diNAH

One of the classic jazz violin cuts of all time. (For Stephane's remarks about his fortuitous meeting with Eddie South, see the complete Grappelli interview on page 22.)

Eddie South and Stephane make perfect foils for one another here. Stephane begins the piece, obviously excited. After four bars of the melody he can no longer restrain himself, and begins a solo full of slides, syncopation, and tritone licks. Eddie comes in after a modulation up to A-flat. This solo is really South at his best; smooth, inventive and incredibly chopsy. Watch out for a tremendous amount of rubato at various places here.

We come back up to G for the trades. Stephane enters first with a phrase filled with South-ern romanticism, and Eddie answers him in the same vein. This cat and mouse game goes on for the next two choruses, and at times, it's very difficult to tell the two fiddlers apart. As a rule, Stephane plays longer lines of eighth-notes with lots of slides into the flatted thirds and sevenths and much more of a driving, swing feeling. Eddie's lines contain less rhythmic motion, but employ an enormous amount of rubato and many quarter-note triplets. In addition, South's bowing often has a *glottal stop* attack, which is heard as a "ping" at the beginning of a note.

The last six bars, are actually much crazier than what's notated here, as Eddie and Stephane are playing simultaneously. I've just extrapolated the basic line that each man plays.

Motifs
1C meas. 7-8 and meas. 70

dinah

Djangologie # 5   EMI-PATHE CO54 16005

Askt, Lewis, and Young

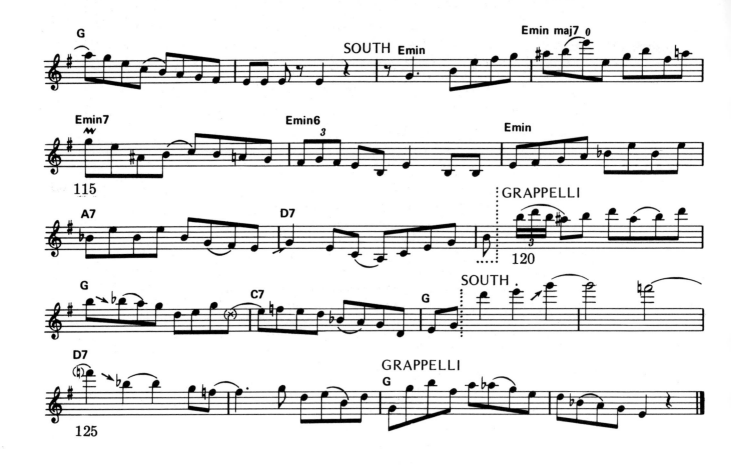

115

120

125

AfTER YOU'VE GONE

Here are two versions of this tune, separated by forty years. The first version is from an incredible 1936 session in which the quintet was joined by guest vocalist Freddie Taylor.

Stephane, (wearing a mute) kicks off the performance with a perfunctory nod to the melody, about three notes worth, and then he's off. The entire performance reminds me of something that Grappelli said to jazz writer Whitney Balliet of the *New Yorker*. "Improvisation, it is a mystery. You can write a book about it, but by the end no one still knows what it is. When I improvise and I'm in good form, I'm like somebody half sleeping. I even forget there are people in front of me. Great improvisers are like priests; they are thinking only of their god."

After Django's guitar solo, Stephane enters with his official improvised break, sans mute. The first chorus has a swooping feeling, with many slides on strong beats and a large number of phrases which cross all four strings. Stephane moves up to sixth position by the end of this chorus where his pseudo-clarinet style passages carry us into the last chorus. The atmosphere becomes predictably frenzied, but **Steph** continues to play with focused legerity. His two-bar break on G (measures 48-49) and the E7/A minor passage (measures 54-55) are especially delicious and Stephane plays here with frightening alacrity. Toward the end, the rhythm becomes more disjunct, and Stephane moves back up the neck where he ends his break on a high B, which is about as high up as he ever goes.

Our second break comes from a 1976 recording made with pianist George Shearing. I chose this version because it has a feeling of bemused repose and differs radically from the barely contained hysteria of the earlier version.

After a peculiar four-bar break, an older and wiser Stephane, does not hesitate to play the melody. The band stops playing for four bars on a G chord while Grappelli outlines a C diminished seventh, an F diminished seventh, and finally a G seventh (measures 17-20).

The second chorus begins with a relaxed, bluesy, melody-derived figure which eases into eighth-notes (measure 21 and on). Aside from a few flat-nine phrases (measures 54 and 63) Steph plays it pretty safe here, meshing in nicely with the conservative Shearing sound.

Motifs
4C meas. 13, 15
4A meas. 33-34, 54-55

(l. to r.) Stephane Grappelli, Eugene Vées, bass player, Django Reinhardt, and Joseph Reinhardt.

After You've Gone I

Djangologie # 2   EMI PATHE CO54 16002

Creamer and Layton

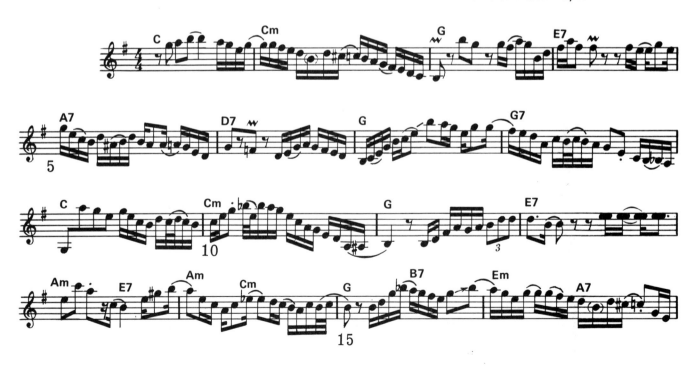

After You've Gone II

The Reunion   MPS DELTA SD 0642 99457

Creamer and Layton

SHINE I

A perfect example of Stephane and the boys making "silver out of schlock." The original "Happy Negro" lyrics are sung here by Freddie Taylor with his tongue planted firmly in his cheek; alternate lyrics were soon to be written which began, "Shine away your bluesies, right down to your shoesies," despite protests from the *American Society for Prevention of Cruelty to Language.*

Django and Stephane didn't speak a word of English at this time and were blissfully unaware of all this. The melody, the chord changes especially, are great for improvising, and everyone sounds as if they're having a swell time. After a broad statement of the melody, Stephane returns with a rhythmic figure reminiscent of his second entrance on "After You've Gone" from the same session. His first chorus contains a lot of rapid-fire sixteenth-notes (too fast to be swung) interspersed with notes of longer duration which he often slides into.

The second chorus begins with a declamatory phrase way up there in sixth position and as the temperature continues to rise, Stephane's phrases become more jagged and chromatic. Also notice how he anticipates some of the chord changes by as much as two bars—(a technique which was popularized much later by guitarist Charlie Christian). Steff repeats a rising scalar motif, three times as a signal that we're near the finish line. The last few bars swing like crazy, leading into a sustained clarinet-like ending. *Wail!*

Motifs
1A meas. 28
1B meas. 30

SHINE I

Djangologie # 2 EMI PATHE CO54 16002

Dabney, Mack, and Brown

Shine II

The same tune, forty years later. This is a perfect example of how Stephane's sense of rhythm has become more and more relaxed as the years have gone by. Here he floats effortlessy through the chord changes and over the bar lines, spinning out endless runs of eighth-notes.

Harmonically, we can see that Stephane has been keeping up with the Joneses, Parkers, and Gillespies. His use of chord substitutions has expanded greatly. In measures 15 and 16, over a G seventh chord, he outlines B-flat, E-flat major seventh, C-sharp diminished, and D.

A musical reminiscence of 1936 occurs in measure 89, where he invokes the spirit of Eddie South by playing one of his favorite *falling-down-stairs* licks.

Motifs
1C meas. 25, 33-4, 47-8,
    56-7, 64, 91
1B meas. 30, 34-5
4A meas. 51-2, 57-8, 72,
    94
2A meas. 35-6
3C meas. 48-9
5E meas. 26-7

Shine II

Violinspiration   MPS BASF MC 22545

Dabney, Mack, and Brown

gliss. Sul G

73

i've found a
new baby I

One of the classic *hot-minor* swing tunes. This first version is transcribed from a dual recording by Django and Stephane. (Other Django duets in the book include "Baby," with Stephane, and "Sweet Georgia Brown," with Eddie South.)

Stephane and Django were a world unto themselves when they played together. Django's uncanny backup guitar created a full and varied counterpart which inspired Stephane to reach new improvisational heights.

Here is a good example of the early Stephane thinking on his feet. The duet form gives him a chance to stretch out (four choruses as opposed to the customary one or two) and allows us to see what a tireless improviser he was even at this early date. Notice the slightly reedy tone and relatively short phrase lengths (which changed with the passage of time) and the use of notes in the upper reaches of the E string for dramatic effect (which hasn't changed).

Motifs
4B meas. 77

i've found a new baby I

Djangologie # 5   EMI PATHE CO54 16005

Palmer and Williams

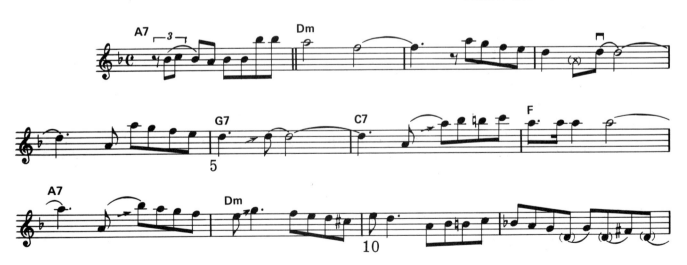

i've found a new baby II

Again we have four choruses of Grappelli on these changes, with the addition of thirty-odd years of practice, and, boy, it shows!

Even at the very fast tempo which Barney Kessel sets, Stephane manages to breeze through his solo, constructing long, arching phrases as if there were no bar lines to worry about. Modern refinements of the Grappelli style include a warm, round tone, increased rhythmic subtlety, and an increased use of motivic improvisation.

Notice the use of harmonics (measure 77) and the retention and employment of a motif used on the earlier version of this tune (4B—measures 69, 98, 107).

Motifs
4B meas. 69, 98, 107
3B meas. 85-89
5C meas. 101
5D meas. 105-106
3A meas. 111-112

i've found a new baby II

I Remember Django   BLACK LION RECORDS AFE BL 105

Palmer and Williams

79

i've found a new baby III

Violently swinging fiddle playing! This is the first cut from an extraordinary album by Venuti with Zoot Sims, *Joe and Zoot* (Chiarosuro CR 128). Joe's statement of the melody establishes him quickly as a man you wouldn't want to mess with in a dark alley. He slashes away at the most important pitch in the melody, A, and its lower neighbor, G, as if possessed. In measures 17 and 18, Venuti uses a three-note rhythmic pattern, something we've discussed elsewhere. (See the analysis of Ponty's "It Don't Mean a Thing" and Venuti's "Undecided.")

In response to a question about improvising, Mr. Venuti once told me that he used his first finger like a capo. What he meant was that he placed his finger on the most important pitch (tonic or temporary tonic) which delineated a full octave of that particular chord. He would play across the strings, within that octave framework just as a guitar player would. (This is in opposition to the classical approach of shifting often to maintain the sound of one string.) This technique of Venuti's is quite evident in this piece especially in measures which include the high F, (played with the pinky in fifth position). It is a very good rule for improvising on the violin, and I guess we can call it "Venuti's Constant"; stay in position whenever possible, and play across the strings.

What you see as the bridge of the last chorus is a very loose approximation of what was actually played; Joe and Zoot were wailing simultaneously and I had a tough time telling them apart.

i've found a new baby III

Joe and Zoot   CHIAROSCURO CR 128

Palmer and Williams

SWEET GEORGIA brown I

If this had been the only recording Eddie South had left to posterity it would still have been enough to insure his position as one of the immortals of jazz violin. The dark, throaty tone, powerful bow attack, and uncanny rhythmic ideas are all in evidence throughout this duet with Django.

South had a unique improvisational style, the hallmarks of which include octave displacement (measures 3 and 59), the insistent repetition of a particular pitch, with myriad changes in the rhythm and approach tones (measures 13, 23, 29 and 30, 37 and 38, 45 and 46, 49 and 50, 53 and 54, 65 and 66) and popping pull-offs which involve the open string (throughout).

SWEET GEORGIA brown I

Djangologie # 5   EMI PATHE CO54 16005

Bernie, Pinkard, and Casey

SWEET GEORGIA brown II

This recording and others from the same period, are ample evidence that Stephane and Django were acutely aware of the be-bop revolution and it's forthcoming changes in musical language. On their recording of "What Is This Thing Called Love" from the same session, they insert a lengthy unison quote from Tadd Dameron's "Hot House," a favorite tune of Charlie Parker's which was only a few years old at the time.

Stephane states the melody here using a tightly-controlled bowing. It also sounds to me as if he's playing with a mute, something he did often in the late forties.

The break is very boppish, and makes wonderful use of space. The highly chromatic measures 26-27 contain a deceptively difficult *walk-up* lick which leads into a heavy triplet-laden passage. Measure 32 has a fifth to third position phrase which is a forerunner of motif 2B.

The last chorus has, among other things, lots of ninths, more triplets, and an unexpected trade with Django. After a final flirtation with the melody, Grappelli takes us out with a lengthy ascending chromatic run.

Motifs
4A meas. 25

SWEET GEORGIA brown II

Djangologie # 17 EMI-PATHE CO54 16017

Bernie, Pinkard, and Casey

baby

A nice, rarely played standard with an "I've Got Rhythm" construction is the scenario for another Django/Stephane duet.

This is from a transitional period in Grappelli's playing, more sophisticated than his earliest recordings, yet not as lush as his modern style. Stephane uses a lighter attack with his bow than he had previously, in order to execute his sixteenth-notes in a more fluid manner. Rhythmically, he is more relaxed and swinging, and harmonically more adventurous. There is heavy use of chromaticism throughout, and some new and interesting arpeggios: augmented (measure 40), major seventh (measure 41), and flat nine (measure 86).

Additionally, there are a lot of unusual licks here, particularly the Louis Armstrong derived phrase in measures 104-107.

baby

Djangologie # 9   EMI-PATHE CO54 16009

McHugh and Fields

91

unDecided I

This simple little melody, and its attendant set of standard chord changes, have proven to be one of the most durable of improvising vehicles. For your pleasure and perusal we have four breaks on this tune; an early Grappelli, two modern Grappellis, and a middle period Venuti.

Our first version comes from a 1939 Hot Club Quintet recording where guest vocalist Beryl Davis does her best to imitate Ella Fitzgerald. Stephane plays a little break, just three-quarters of a chorus, but it's archetypal swing fiddle all the way. Not only is this break rhythmically propelling, but it's harmonically sophisticated to boot. Notice measures 5 and 13, especially where Grappelli outlines a G seven flat-nine arpeggio over a D seven chord. Quarter tones are employed in two places; first in measure 11, where Steph plays a note slightly below B-flat, and then again in measure 21, where he achieves a clarinet-like effect by alternating between an E-natural and a lower neighbor a quarter-tone away.

Motif
5D meas. 7

unDecided I

Parisian Swing GNP CRESCENDO 9002

Shavers and Robin

The next two choruses are from a pleasant 1971 outing entitled *Afternoon in Paris*. They are included because of Stephane's genteel reading of the melody, with subtle alterations at the end of each phrase, and for the unhurried improvisation which follows.

Motifs
1B meas. 15-16
5D meas. 23-24
5E meas. 33-34
1C meas. 37-38, 61
3A meas. 50-52

undecided II

Afternoon in Paris   MPS 20876

Shavers and Robin

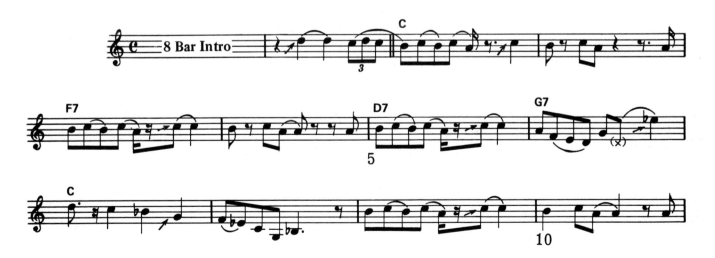

UNDECIDED III

In sharp contrast to the former, relaxed version, our final Grappelli break on this tune is incendiary. It's taken from a 1969 recording with Barney Kessel, where Steph plays three burning choruses without a let-up.

Here again we can see Grappelli's use of motivic improvising as a device to keep the heat up on a high speed tune. This break uses far more of our classified motifs than anything else in the book, but don't be deceived; Grappelli's not just playing licks. These motifs are the building blocks of Stephane's improvisational style, and he uses more of them here because he has that much more to say. They generate one another in a kaleidoscopic manner and if for some reason they don't, Steph will latch on to a melodic fragment, repeat it a few times, and turn that into a new motif.

At one point, things get so wild that Grappelli and the rhythm section temporarily part ways. This happens around measure 61, and things stay slightly out of sync until the C seventh chord at measure 81 repairs the schism.

Motifs
1A meas. 2-bar pick-up,
      35-36, 40-41, 68-69,
      74-76, 94-96
1B meas. 91
1C meas. 5-6, 70-71
2A meas. 12-13, 92
2B meas. 14, 33
2C meas. 53-55
3A meas. 19-20
3B meas. 66-67, 81-83
4A meas. 11-12, 37-38
4C meas. 8-9
5B meas. 33-34
5C meas. 43-44

undecided III

Limehouse Blues AFE-BL-173

Shavers and Robin

gliss. Sul G

UNdecided IV

Joe Venuti had a big band for a short while in the forties, and his break on "Undecided" comes from the only available recording by this aggregation. Joe has a long history of playing in bands with lots of horns, and he really knew how to lean into his bow to produce a sound as big as all outdoors. On those old Boswell Sisters or Paul Whiteman records Joe can be heard, not yet amplified, clear as day, floating on top of the dense orchestrations.

Venuti's improvisational approach to this tune and his style in general, could hardly be more different than Stephane's. Although this is a gross generalization, we could say that where Grappelli is "Mr. Melody," Joe was "Mr. Rhythm." Venuti was a power player; an unflagging swinger. "Joe could make the chandelier swing," a famous horn player once remarked.

In terms of his harmonic outlook, Venuti dealt mostly with arpeggios, broken chords and other vertical structures in the same way Grappelli uses melody and a linear approach in his improvising. This characteristic of Joe's playing is evident here. He enters with a trumpet-like triplet rendering of the tonic chord which turns into a three-note rhythmic pattern on the same arpeggio. As the pattern moves through the four-beat measures, different notes are emphasized and a highly syncopated figure is the result.

Ex: *Ve*-nu-ti Ve/*nu*-ti-Ven-nu/*ti*-Ve-nu-ti/etc:

For a longer discussion of these rhythmic patterns see the analysis of Jean-Luc Ponty's solo on "It Don't Mean a Thing (If it Ain't Got that Swing)."

This rhythmic pattern becomes a mini-motif as variants of it occur at measure 12 and again at measure 27. Another standard Venuti device is his use of high tessitura clarinet-derived lines. These passages occur at measures 5, 9, 17, and 25. In measure 20, Joe slides up to the natural harmonic two octaves above his open A string, moves over to his D string to play the same harmonic there, and slides down again.

undecided IV

Joe Venuti and his Big Band   GOLDEN ERA RECORDS LP 1506(1)

Shavers and Robin

alabamy bound

"Alabamy Bound" is a good example of Stephane burning it up at high speeds. After a secure statement of the melody, Grappelli leaps into his first improvised chorus with one of the hottest two-bar breaks I've ever heard him take. This little phrase consists of an ascending diminished arpeggio connected to a descending chromatic scale with a nice, "Look Ma, no bar lines," feeling.

The solo itself is a breathless, headlong rush of sixteenth notes with occasional pauses for Stephane and his listeners to catch their collective breaths.

Stephane makes use of motivic improvisation at a number of places here, (always a good device on very up-tempo tunes). Beginning in measure 40, measure 50, and again at measure 54 in the first chorus, and at measure 75 and then measure 83 in the second chorus, a motivic germ is developed into an idea.

Motifs
4C meas. 31
2B meas. 45
3B meas. 83-4
1B meas. 93-4

Alabamy bound

Stephane Grappelli   EVEREST FS 311

DeSylva, Green, and Henderson

SWEET
Lorraine

This is not a ballad, but it's the closest we come to one in this book. Stephane states the melody freely, virtually floating over the bar lines. *Grappelli harmonics* appear at the end of measure 24. Shortly thereafter, Stephane glides smoothly into double time, at the pickup to measure 30. The second chorus has great emotional intensity, with high register playing and more double time passages which start at measure 37 and go to the end.

Stephane executes a *double-doink* over the first beat-and-a-half of measure 46 (no, that's not a ballet dancer's move). The realization for this B-flat should be *da-oo-ah-oo-ah*.

Motifs
1B meas. 14
4A meas. 15, 30
2C meas. 30, 31

SWEET Lorraine

Violinspiration MPS BASF MC 22545

Parish and Burwell

i CAN'T believe i
(THAT YOU'RE iN love wiTH ME)

This lovely standard seems to have become one of Stephane's favorite tunes within the last few years; he has recorded it numerous times and often opens his sets with it.

I've chosen to include two modern versions of the tune which are very different in character. The first, from the Angel recording *Jalousie—Music of the Thirties,* could be thought of as the *tight* version, whereas the second from *Les Grandes Violinistes de Jazz* is the *loose* one. A qualitative difference in rhythmic feel is responsible for the contrast between the two versions.

The tempo of the first version is faster than that of the second; this element, combined with the motion of the rhythm section, causes Steph to play on top of the beat with an energetic, driving approach. Throughout his two improvised choruses, Stephane sounds as if he's straining at the bit. He unleashes a torrent of vigorous eighth-notes and triplets which come to rest only in the last beautifully constructed measure. Watch out for the ascending E eleventh arpeggio in measure 49 and the artificial harmonics in measure 84.

Motifs
5A meas. 37-38
4A meas. 39, 72, 86-87
2A meas. 42
2B meas. 43-44
5B meas. 45
1A meas. 46-48
1B meas. 60, 85, 93, 94-5
5C meas. 73-74

i CAN'T bElİEVE İ
(THAT yOU'RE İN LOVE WİTH ME)

Jalousie—Music of the Thirties ANGEL SFO 36968

Gaskill and McHugh

i CAN'T
believe II
(THAT YOU'RE IN LOVE WITH ME)

The tempo of our second version is slower, the rhythm section feel is funkier and Stephane plays behind the beat with a laconic swagger. Grappelli plays the melody with such conviction that one can easily forget that bar lines exist. He then launches into two harmonically adventurous choruses which emanate great joy. There is free use of rubato here, and many phrases have a quarter-note triplet feeling. (Be careful of the one in measure 45 which crosses the bar line.) The two measures beginning at measure 57 are an indecipherable blur of notes and, as with similar passages in the Ponty transcriptions, you should listen to the recording until your ear becomes acclimated to the style.

The improvisation in the second chorus becomes slightly more heated, with forays into the higher registers. However, Grappelli continues to maintain the seamless quality established earlier on. Toward the end, he throws in some uncharacteristic bebop phrases, beginning with a flat-nine arpeggio in measure 87 and including a fragment of a diminished scale in measure 90.

Motifs
1C meas. 29-30, 61-62
3C meas. 37-38, 75
5B meas. 65-66
1A meas. 67-68, 72
1B meas. 85

i can't believe ii
(that you're in love with me)

Les Grandes Violinistes de Jazz   PHILIPS 1B6612-039

Gaskill and McHugh

SWEET SUE

"Sweet Sue" was one of the four tunes that Stephane and Django played on their first recording session in 1934 for Raoul Caldione of Ultrafox. It's only fitting, then, that Stephane should have recorded it again on his *Homage to Django* album nearly forty years later.

Once again, the modern version of an older tune illustrates Stephane's increasing tendency to relax rhythmically when he plays and incorporate new harmonic ideas.

Grappelli's playing on this cut is astonishingly relaxed and fluid, one idea generates the next with absolutely no sharp edges. "The movement is like water you see, you don't know where the water goes. I always visualize that."

Stephane plays two graceful choruses in F before Marc Hemmler's piano solo. He reenters with a two octave ascending scale, which leads into a motivic phrase based on a descending suspended minor seventh. In measure 87, there's an E-flat diminished arpeggio over a D chord, and subsequently, (at measure 90) a "Parkerish" phrase employing the sharp-nine, flat-nine alternation.

The final chorus kicks up to G and finds Stephane exploring the higher registers of the fiddle, especially in measures 118 and 119.

Motifs
5E meas. 33
1B meas. 61, 101
4A meas. 131
2C meas. 135, 140

Stephane Grappelli

SWEET SUE

Homage to Django CLASSIC JAZZ 23

Harris and Young

PONTY INTERVIEW

Jean-Luc Ponty is largely responsible for the renaissance of jazz violin. Born September 29, 1942 in Avranches, France, Ponty began to study the violin at the age of five with his father. At fifteen he entered the Paris Conservatory and subsequently graduated with that institute's Premier Prix. It was around this time that Ponty fell madly in love with jazz. Although a brilliant classical violinist with a secure future ahead of him, Jean-Luc opted instead for the precarious life of a jazz musician. In the following interview he describes how he accomplished this difficult crossover.

Matt Glaser: *How did you make the transition from classical music to jazz?*

Jean-Luc Ponty: *At first I was playing along with albums of Grappelli, and after a few months I discovered Stuff Smith—I went crazy over him—he was the most revolutionary; he played the violin with so much punch. Grappelli and Stuff were my first two influences.*

MG *What was your first exposure to bebop?*

JLP *I had an album by Stuff Smith where he was accompanied by* The Oscar Peterson Trio. *I mean, I was listening as much to Oscar Peterson's solos as I was to Stuff, and soon I was trying to play those licks on the violin.*

Jean-Luc Ponty

MG *How old were you at this time?*

JLP *17 or 18.*

MG *Had you met Stephane at this time?*

JLP *No. Let me go back a little ways. I was a student at the* Conservatoire de Musique *in Paris studying classical violin. At the same time I was playing in an amateur jazz band at a local polytechnic institute. This jazz band needed a clarinet player and I played clarinet as a third instrument, after the piano. I went down there for the fun of it; because I didn't know what jazz was about at that time. I thought that classical music was the only serious music—I thought my future vocation would be as a conductor. Getting my violin degree was to be a first step—then I wanted to study composition and conducting. So, I didn't know exactly what jazz meant—I sort of equated pop music with jazz, I didn't know the difference. Well, that band taught me the rudiments of jazz—that improvisation was involved in the basic rules of the jazz discipline. I learned how to follow a tune, how to improvise on chord changes.*

I was going there once or twice a month on Sundays; we'd play for parties on weekends. It was a treat for me to go out and meet girls, to get out of the classical conservatory atmosphere and to party.

One day I got a gig as a classical violinist in a small city in the south of France; I was to play a sonata on the radio and a concerto with the local orchestra. On Saturday night there I was really bored and someone told me that the New Orleans clarinetist Albert Nicholas was playing in a local club. So I went with a friend; I had my violin because I'd just gotten out from my gig. That was the first time I'd heard a black American musician live; before this, my only exposure to jazz was playing clarinet in that band.

I got so excited that I wanted to go onstage and jam with them. At first I thought of asking the guy to borrow his clarinet, but I knew that wouldn't be possible, so I decided to go up with my violin, which I had never done before. So I jammed with the band, with my violin, and at the time I had never heard of jazz violin or Grappelli or Stuff. I was about 16 at this time. I got so excited and the audience got so excited that it was a real thrill. I knew how to improvise on the melody of basic standard jazz tunes; however, I had never done it on violin and the excitement it generated was thrilling.

The bandleader of the local band who was backing up Nicholas came to me afterwards and said, "Who are you? Where are you from?" So I told him that I was a young classical violinist studying at the Conservatory in Paris. He said, "Why don't you come to my house?" So the next day I went to his house and this guy did a jazz radio program and he had thousands of records. He had an entire rack labelled "Jazz Violin." That's how I learned of Grappelli, Eddie South, Venuti, Stuff Smith. After this incident I went through all the record stores in Paris looking for albums of jazz violin. I realized that it was something that existed, even though I had discovered it by accident. I realized that there were masters that existed in that field. So I tried to get albums, but they were very scarce; it was hard to get any albums except for the many albums by Grappelli and Django Reinhardt and a few by Stuff Smith.

So, I started playing along with Grappelli and Stuff Smith albums, assimilating their styles. But very fast I was attracted by more contempo-

rary style jazz. When I heard Oscar Peterson, you know, from then on I got into Clifford Brown and the bebop school, and almost six months later I was into Miles Davis. Thereafter, I wanted to play more like Miles, Coltrane, and Charlie Parker than the older style violinists.
That's when I started shaping my own style, influenced by keyboard players, horn players etc. I wanted to sound like a trumpet or a horn.

MG   Did you learn specific solos?

JLP   No. I never studied a specific solo, to write it down and try to play it—I never did that in my life.
What I was doing was jamming along with the albums, but trying to do my own solos, my own lines.
At this time classical music was still my main activity—I had to graduate from school so I was working very hard on my classical stuff. It was only after I graduated and got my diploma that I took off, free, and started hanging out in jazz clubs in Paris and jamming around. That's when I really started being involved, more and more with jazz.
I got an engagement right away with one of the best symphony orchestras in Paris, but I was still jamming at night in the jazz clubs. I mean, I was listening to albums like crazy, it was the only way to learn. I would wake up and listen to albums all day long and play along with them.
Just by hearing the phrasing and accentuation—a mixture of detaché and slurs which would give that bebop sound.

MG   Did you experiment with specific bowings to see which ones would communicate that style best, or did it just evolve naturally?

JLP   It was natural. I didn't try to analyze the technique—to say, "Okay, I'm going to practice these bowings"; I just played along with records and let it come naturally.
At first it wasn't natural—all my notes were too even, more like Bach. There wasn't enough syncopation. It was mostly by jamming with professional jazz players in Paris—a few guys who really loved me were telling me what was wrong with my playing—they were real friends. When you love someone you want to correct them.
I was getting a lot of attention. I would come from my classical concert where I was playing Stravinsky and all that music, which was very impressive to some jazz musicians. I would come down to the club and I'd be able to improvise—I knew all the rules. I was very well received; I was looked on as an oddity. There were a few guys, however, one or two, who'd say, "Look, what you're doing is fantastic, but you're still a bit classical in your rhythmic approach," and they'd point me in the right direction.

MG   So, your acquisition of a jazz language on the violin came mostly from playing with other people?

JLP   Right, more from live experience. I never tried to apply too much of my technical knowledge. It was only later on, once I had found that easiness and flow with the bowing, that I began to think about what I could apply of my technical knowledge, to go further and to add more. In 1973, for the first time in my life, I did a workshop at a school in Salt Lake City. They had jazz classes for strings; they were asking me,

"How do you phrase bebop, what kind of bowing do you use?" I wasn't able to tell them because I'd never analyzed what I was doing. So I said, "Okay, I'll play and you look at it and tell me what I'm doing," and I realized then that all that bebop style playing was a variety of short slurs, (two notes slurred together), and a few detaché strokes, changing to vary the accents.

I would say that the first basic principle of bebop bowing, and this is something Grappelli does a lot, is to slur from the offbeat to the next downbeat— ♪♪♪♪♪ —(da)-da-oh-da-oh-da-oh. So you have that a lot in bebop, but with more variety of detaché.

MG At what point did you meet Grappelli?

JLP Very quickly after I started playing around Paris my name came to his ear. In fact, it was through the son of Django Reinhardt. He was, like his father, a guitar player, although more modern. We met and went to his caravan outside Paris and jammed. Being the son of Django, he kept contact with Grappelli and one day he told me that Grappelli would like me to come and meet him. So I did so, and was very excited. Grappelli took me to a club and had me jam, and listened to me. He told me I was very talented, that I had an original style and I should go on. At that time I didn't know whether I should pursue jazz as a hobby or a profession. I didn't know what to expect for my future.

MG What were your parent's feelings?

JLP They didn't know much about it and they didn't care. I'd completed my obligations towards them—I'd gotten my diploma and secured my future in classical music if I wanted. They sure had spent a lot of money and sacrificed their own lives. Being from a small town, they had to send me to Paris when I was fifteen and I'd only see them three times a year. So it was an emotional as well as financial sacrifice.

My father had made a pact with me that I wouldn't touch any other kind of music until I'd finished my classical studies. It's like he had prophesized—at the time I didn't know why he was saying that, but later on it really happened.

I was really pulled toward jazz more and more but nevertheless I didn't know whether I should take the chance and leave classical music. But meeting Grappelli, and him telling me that, well that really impressed me. Coming from him, who was an established, recognized giant of the jazz violin. I have always appreciated his help; he's been great.

MG About this time you were playing with mainstream jazz groups around Paris?

JLP Yes. And I was called about Europe. I did my first solo album when I was twenty-one. It was called Jean-Luc Ponty—Jazz Long Playing. The record was very bebop. I played a few Charlie Parker tunes and a few originals by French jazz musicians. I have one piece of my own on that record—something in 6/8 or 3/4—it was really avant-garde for jazz at that time. I was so hot, technically, out of the conservatory and I had assimilated that bebop phrasing so well, that I'm still impressed by that record now. Of course, it sounds like a young boy to me—when I hear that record it's like I'm looking at a picture of myself when I was very *young, but, nevertheless, it was very good bebop. It was around this time that I stopped using vibrato; I was listening to Miles and Coltrane and I wanted to emulate Trane's sound.*

MG *You mentioned that you had a composition of your own on that first album. Had you been composing a lot up until that time?*

JLP *No, that was really my first. . .well, when I was young I would write little things for fun, like a piece in the style of Bach, and a piece for clarinet. When I got into jazz it took me a while to start writing because the sound was so fresh in my ears. The first piece of mine that I recorded was in 6/8, but it sounded like 4/4 because the melody was on the dotted quarter notes. It was sort of a pizzicato duet with bass where I'd play a double stop and the bass would play one note so that we'd get a chord. It was pretty strange.*
When I really started composing I had difficulty playing my compositions with people because it was always an odd number of bars. My pieces were very melodic with strange chord progressions for jazz, very impressionistic. It might have a fourteen bar form where most jazz tunes at the time were very square, very even. The chords wouldn't necessarily change every bar or every two bars—they might change after an odd number of bars. All this was obviously, although I didn't know it at the time, the effect of my classical training. It was very hard for me to break out of that tradition and establish jazz ties. And that's how I got to where I am today. A few years ago I decided not to bother with the conventions of jazz, and just to write my own music, not caring if it sounded like jazz, or anything else.

MG *When did you start playing electric, as opposed to just amplified, violin?*

JLP *Two years after the* Sunday Walk *album I met John Berry of Barcus-Berry in California and he gave me an electric violin. At the same time, 1969-70, there were a lot of electronic devices being invented– Echoplex and others, and I started to experiment with them.*
When I first played at a jam session when I was eighteen I realized that I couldn't play without amplification, so I bought an amp. The tone I was getting through the amp was so different, and I got a kick out of it, I liked it. It helped me play jazz actually, because it took me away from that traditional violin sound. Even on Sunday Walk *where it's a regular violin, but amplified, the sound in the lower register is fatter, rounder. So amplification helped me develop an individual sound.*
As I said, it wasn't until the late sixties, early seventies, that I consciously decided to work with electronics. I wanted to help give the electric violin an identity of it's own. I had also opened my ears to rock. I had an affinity with progressive rock musicians; we shared a curiousity for new sound, electric sounds. I had found a tendency among jazz musicians to be conservative, almost reactionary. They didn't want to deal with electricity. I didn't have that attitude at all; I'd always been very open, otherwise I wouldn't have chosen to play jazz in the first place. So I started to find the same conservatism among jazz musicians as I had found among classical musicians previously, and I didn't want to deal with that. I had always been thrilled with new sounds. Having an electric violin allowed me to plug in the same devices as a guitar player or a keyboard player. That's how I started to experiment with all these devices.

MG   *Can you tell me something about the making of the first* Violin Summit *record?*

JLP   *Well, that was a thrill for me. I was not yet as well known as they were. They were all established jazz violinists, and that was the beginning of my career. To be on stage with those masters was an incredible thrill for me, and at the same time, a chance for me to burn, and prove myself, to them and to the audience. I was twenty-three then (1966) and I'd been playing jazz professionally for two years.*
Well, we did the concert in the early evening and that was recorded, but the producer felt that there were some things that could have been better, so he wanted us to record all the tunes again in a studio. Stuff Smith was so drunk that he couldn't go, and we had to wait for him to sleep a few hours; so about three or four A.M. he woke up and was in great shape—refreshed, ready for a new day, but the rest of us were all worn out! And finally, of course, what came out from the studio was lousy. It had none of the magic of the live concert.

MG   *Do you ever play classical music anymore?*

JLP   *Yes, I do, at home, never in public. I've always practiced from the same book of scales that I used in the Paris Conservatory, the Sevcik book. And I practice bow technique, although not so much anymore. I've developed my own bow exercises, and I've also developed exercises for warming up my fingers. I've broadened the spectrum of bowings that I use in my own music. For instance, to play bebop, it's very limited, you only use a short section of the bow, as I said before, short slurs and detaché. But even when I was playing bebop I began to use more of the frog. Today, in my own music I use staccato, sautillé, and other very fast bowings like in classical music. What I've been trying to do for the last couple of years is to get away from short-bow bebop phrasing and rather, make long phrases with long bows, more melodic. The left hand can be running like crazy and I'll still use a long-bow stroke.*

MG   *Do you have a practice regimen that you do daily?*

JLP   *Yes, when I can. I don't practice every day anymore, especially when I'm on the road, but I always make sure to warm up thoroughly. Off the road, I try to do an hour or so daily. Etudes, scales, double-stops, Paganini. Nowadays in my music, I can blend bebop phrasing with all sorts of classical techniques.*

MG   *Do you keep contact with classical music and older styles of jazz?*

JLP   *I still love classical music and I listen to a lot of it when I'm at home. I was very excited to do that TV show with Itzhak Perlman, and we became good friends. In fact, I saw him a couple of weeks ago, and he told me he's going to cut a jazz album. André Previn is going to play piano and write out all the solos.*

MG   *Can Perlman play with a jazz feel?*

JLP   *Well, he's worried about it, but I think Previn is writing the parts out in such a way that they'll fit the rhythm section—Ray Brown, Shelly*

Manne. I know Itzhak would like to do something with me.

As far as old jazz is concerned. . .I don't have much time. I have to select my schedule every day. I have so much to do, the pressure is very heavy— I can't do everything I want. Soon I hope to get off the road, relax, and prepare an album without any deadline at all. Anyway, I still love to listen to Oscar Peterson, McCoy Tyner, but I'm so involved with what I'm doing now, I don't have much desire to play that music myself.

MG Do you have any advice for young violin players who want to play jazz?

JLP It's hard to give advice. When you look at the careers of the great jazz violinists, we all came from different backgrounds and took totally different paths. My classical technique was, at first, a handicap to getting into jazz, but once I got rid of the stiffness, it turned out to be an advantage because I was able to evolve towards the type of music I wanted to play, thanks to that technique. Although talent and imagination are the most important ingredients for an artist, the maximum technique will help carry it out.

It's most important to be original. Learn from your predecessors, and then apply that knowledge in a new creation.

Appendix

Here are a number of extra transcriptions.

The modern Grappelli versions of "It Don't Mean a Thing (If it Ain't Got that Swing)" and "Sweet Georgia Brown" were transcribed and analyzed by Joe Weed. Joe is a violinist, composer and writer from California who was kind enough to donate some of his fine work to this book. Keep your eyes open for a forthcoming folio by Joe containing other jazz violin transcriptions with analyses.

It Don't Mean A Thing II (if it ain't got that swing)

Grappelli recorded "It Don't Mean a Thing" in 1973, and while this represents a passage of almost twenty-five years since his work with Django Reinhardt, his approach still remains basically the same, and his style is still quite identifiable—that of a *play-over-the-changes* swing musician. The current Grappelli, however, is more fluid, more inventive harmonically, and freer with his construction of phrases, which often tend to be longer.

An important element of Grappelli's sound is his phrasing. Notice in the first "A" section (measures 1-8) how he quickly climbs up, then gradually works his way down until in measure 8 he zig-zags up through the turnaround chord to repeat the process for the second "A" section (measures 9-16). The bridge works up to a swinging quarter-note section (measure 18), then smoothly dips and rises, until in the return to the final "A" section, the high point of energy occurs near the end (measures 20-29).

Some examples of good, typical swing outlining of changes can be found in measures 7-8 (vi-ii-V-I) and also in measures 17-20 (ii-V-I).

The return to the melody is a good device which brings a new orientation and fresh start to a solo. Grappelli hints at it as he starts his second chorus (measures 33-36) and returns to it as he is drawing his solo to a close (measures 57-65).

Motivic or pattern development can be found in measures 10-11, 49-50, and 84-87. This type of development can help tie things together, to give the solo a more integral sound. In measures 49-50 and 84-87 the *off-the-beat* rhythmic orientation is maintained through the pattern's repetitions.

Grappelli uses some altered tones to give the music added bite. Note the use of the flatted fifth over the dominant chord in measures 8 and 70. The flatted fifth is superimposed over the minor tonic chord in measures 26-27, 43-44, and 97, and over a major tonic in measure 37. The use of the G harmonic minor scale over the D seven flat-nine dominant chord works very well, and emphasizes the flatted ninth and diminished sounds. See measures 39-40, 93-94, 101-102, and 117-118. The diminished seventh arpeggios in measures 39-40 and 115-116 give a similar effect. The major seventh over a dominant F chord in measure 85 is used to help set up a whole-tone sound in the descending phrase in measures 84-87.

it don't mean a thing II
(if it ain't got that swing)

Stephane Grappelli – Bill Coleman CLASSIC JAZZ CJ 24

Duke Ellington

SWEET GEORGIA bROWN III

Although Grappelli has recorded and performed this old standard countless times, he still brings a fine buoyant spirit and a relaxed light touch to this version, recorded live in London in 1971. His constant use of syncopation is a large factor in the feel he achieves and several examples will be pointed out below.

Grappelli opens his solo with a swinging version of the melody, and here, as in the return in his last chorus (begining in measure 138), he enhances it rhythmically through lots of light syncopation. His break in measures 21-24 employs chromaticism and rhythmic variation with the triplets and ends with a hint of the dominant in measure 24.

Measures 41-44 illustrate a perfect outline of a dominant 13th chord.

Another device which Grappelli likes to use to add color to his lines is the occasional use of parallel fifths (see measures 42-43, 57-60, 105-109, and other solos). These are easily obtained on the violin by stopping adjacent strings with one finger. Since the strings are tuned in fifths, parallel lines result.

Some examples of Grappelli's syncopation may be found in measure 47 (the line starts on an accented up-beat), and in measures 53 and 54 (here the echo, in measure 54, is more effectively syncopated because it doesn't go back up on the accented third beat, as does the line in measure 53). In measures 77 and 78 an echo with the accent on a different beat gives a syncopated feel; the run beginning on beat four of measure 84 starts on an up-beat; in measure 115 the jump to a high Db anticipates beat two and gives both a rhythmic and melodic surprise.

Notice the chromaticism in the phrase from measures 49-52, and especially in the break over measures 150-153.

SWEET GEORGIA bROWN III

Stephane Grappelli Recorded Live at the Queen Elizabeth Hall, London
PYE 12123

Bernie, Pinkard, and Casey

GROOVIN' HIGH

"Groovin' High" is included as an example of pure bebop violin playing, something which is pretty rare.

Ekek Bacsik is a Roumanian gypsy who has played guitar and violin in musical situations as diverse as Las Vegas show bands, Dizzy Gillespie's group and Slavic folk music orchestras. Along the way, he's absorbed enough of Bird's language to make him one of the few bop fiddlers around.

This is Dizzy's bop anthem, based on the chord changes of "Whispering."

Violin Summit, (l. to r.) Stephane Grappelli, Svend Asmussen, Ray Nance, and Duke Ellington (seated).

GROOVIN' HIGH

Bird and Dizzy — A Musical Tribute   FLYING DUTCHMAN BDLI 1082

Dizzy Gillespie

CAT COACH

Although outside of the initial scope of our inquiry, I've included this transcription because it shows the direction in which a standard playing fiddler went immediately after he stopped played standards.

This tune, from Ponty's *Sunday Walk* album, is a complex, modal, open-ended affair in $\frac{3}{4}$. Jean-Luc's improvisation employs some of the same devices he used a year earlier at the Violin Summit, but the nature of this tune allows him to explore improvisation on a deeper level. The more modern interval of a fourth seems to predominate, although beboppish phrases (as if through a fun-house mirror) do rear their heads occasionally (A-25-26, B-19-20). Ponty uses a number of rhythmic motifs here, (the triplet seems to be a common one) with an added twist. He'll often accelerate them logarhythmically until they turn into a supersaturated sheet of sound (A-19-23, B-11-25).

I'd say it's an absolute necessity that you have a recording of this to make heads or tails of it.

CAT COACH

Sunday Walk   PA USA 7033 (MPS)

Wolfgang Dauner

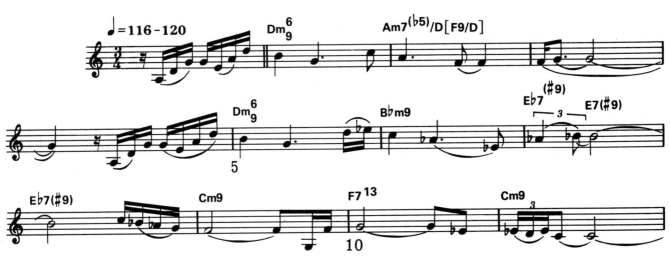

discoqRAPhy

Here is a small, representative sampling of some jazz violin records which are still in print.

Svend Asmussen

Hot Swing Fiddle Classics
Folklyric Records 9025

Toots and Svend/Yesterday and Today
A & M   SP 3613

Svend Asmussen/Amazing Strings
MPS   20 22373 6 (import)

Svend Asmussen Spielt Welterfolge
Telefunken   Musik für alle
NT 421 (import)

Duke Ellington's Jazz Violin Session
Atlantic SD 1688

Stephane Grappelli

(Note: Stephane Grappelli has over one hundred albums currently in print, in the United States and Europe; consult a Schwann catalog for further information!)

Djangologie #1 – 20/Stephane Grappelli with Django Reinhardt
EMI Pathé   CO54 16001 through 16020
also on GNP Crescendo 9001, 9002, 9018, 9019

Stephane Grappelli
Everest FS   311

Stephane Grappelli/Homage to Django
Classic Jazz 23

Stephane Grappelli/ Afternoon in Paris
MPS   20876

Stephane Grappelli
Pye 12115

Stephane Grappelli/I Hear Music
RCA Victor   730107

Stephane Grappelli/Steff and Slam
Black and Blue 33.076

Stephane Grappelli/The Talk of the Town
Black Lion   313 stereo

Stephane Grappelli/Recorded Live at the Queen Elizabeth Hall, London
Pye 12123

Stephane Grappelli
Pye 12135

Stephane Grappelli/Satin Doll
Vanguard   VSD 81/82

Stephane Grappelli Plays Cole Porter
Festival   240

Stephane Grappelli Plays George Gershwin
Festival   205

Stephane Grappelli/I Got Rhythm
Black Lion   047 stereo

Stephane Grappelli/Le Toit de Paris
RCA Victor   740.038

Stephane Grappelli/ Violinspiration
MPS   MC 22545

Stephane Grappelli and Barney
Kessel/I Remember Django
Black Lion 105

Stephane Grappelli and Barney
Kessel/Limehouse Blues
Black Lion 173

Stephane Grappelli—Bill Coleman
Classic Jazz 24

Stephane Grappelli/Grand Gala
Special
Exclusive   Ste 6201

Stephane Grappelli and The
George Shearing Trio/The
Reunion
MPS   5D0642   99457

Stephane Grappelli and Oscar
Peterson
Prestige   24041

Stephane Grappelli and Yehudi
Menuhin/Jalousie—Music of the
Thirties
Angel SFO   36968

Stephane Grappelli and Yehudi
Menuhin/Tea for Two
Angel S   37533

Stephane Grappelli/Uptown
Dance
Columbia 35415

Stephane Grappelli/I Remember
Django
Black Lion Records AFE BL 105

Stephane Grappelli/Parisian Swing
GNP Crescendo 9002

Stephane Grappelli/Homage to
Django
Classic Jazz CJ 23

Jean-Luc Ponty

Violin Summit (with Asmussen,
Grappelli, Stuff)
EMI MPS 5C 064 61227 (import)

Les Grandes Violinistes de Jazz
(with Grappelli)
Philips   6612 039

Sunday Walk
PA USA 7033 (MPS)

More Then Meets the Ear
World Pacific Jazz   St 20134

Electric Connection
World Pacific Jazz   St 20156

Canteloupe Island
Blue Note   LA632   H2

Upon the Wings of Music
Atlantic SD 18138

Aurora
Atlantic SD 18163

Imaginary Voyage
Atlantic SD 18195

Jean-Luc Ponty and Stephane
Grappelli
Inner City 1005

Stuff Smith

Black Violin
MPS 20650

Stuff Smith
Everest FS 238

Hot Swing Fiddle Classics
Folklyric 9025

Violin Summit (see Ponty)

There are also some great out of
print Stuff records that you
should keep your eyes open for,
including:

Have Violin, Will Swing
Verve MGV 8282

Stuff Smith
Verve MGV 8206

Dizzy Gillespie/Stuff Smith
Verve MGV 8214

Also appears on *The Changing Face of Harlem, Vol. 2*
Arista Savoy 2224
(3 great cuts)

Eddie South

Djangologie #5 and #6
EMI Pathé C054 16005
and C054 16006

The Dark Angel of the Fiddle
Trip TLP 5803

Joe Venuti

Stringing the Blues
Columbia CL 1926

Hot Strings
RCA Black and White
Vol. 118 FPMI 7016

Venuti—Lang/1927-1928
The Old Masters TOM 8

Venuti—Lang/1929-1930
The Old Masters TOM 7

Benny Goodman and the Giants of Swing
Prestige 7644

The Radio Years
London HMG 5023

Louis Armstrong/All Star Dates 1947-1950
Alamac QSR 2436

Welcome Joe
Durium msA77356

Joe Venuti in Milan
Durium msA77277

Sliding By
Sonet SNTF 734

Joe Venuti and George Barnes/ Gems
Concord Jazz 14

Joe Venuti and George Barnes/ Live at the Concord Summer Festival
Concord Jazz 30

The Maestro and Friend/with Marian McPartland
Halcyon 112

Nightwings/with Bucky Pizzarelli
Flying Dutchman BDL1 1120

S'Wonderful
Flying Fish 035

In Chicago, 1978
Flying Fish 077

Joe and Zoot
Chiaroscuro 128

Joe Venuti Blue Four
Chiaroscuro 134

Hot Sonatas with Earl Hines
Chiaroscuro 145

Hooray for Joe
Chiaroscuro 153

Alone at the Palace with Dave McKenna
Chiaroscuro 160

Joe Venuti and his Big Band
Golden Era Records LP 1506(1)

Elek Bacsik

Bird and Dizzy/A Musical Tribute
Flying Dutchman BDLI 1082